A Short History of English Schools
1750–1965

Christopher Martin, an Oxford M.A.,
teaches at a Cambridgeshire village college
and supervises History of Education
students at Cambridge University. He is the
author of four Wayland history books,
including *Battle of the Somme* and *English
Life in the First World War*

A Short History of

English Schools

1750 ~ 1965

Christopher Martin

Education is the art of forming children into happy and useful men ... One of the last and most perfect productions of the human mind will be a complete system of education.
David Williams:
A Treatise on Education (1774)

What has the history of education always been? A series of little teaching chaps trying to follow up and fix the fluctuating boundaries of communities like an insufficient supply of upholsterers trying to overtake and tack down a carpet that was blowing away in front of a gale. An insufficient supply of upholsterers ... and the carpet always growing as it blows ...
H. G. Wells:
Joan and Peter (1918)

First published in 1979 by
Wayland Publishers Limited
49 Lansdowne Place, Hove
East Sussex BN3 1HF, England

© Copyright 1979 Christopher Martin

ISBN 0 85340 669 3

Phototypeset by
Computacomp (UK) Ltd, Fort William, Scotland
Printed and bound in England by
R. J. Acford, Chichester

Contents

List of illustrations

Front cover "Two nations": an Eton schoolboy and working-class boys outside Lord's Cricket Ground in the 1930s. This detail from a *Picture Post* photograph sums up what R. H. Tawney called "the organization on lines of class which is the tragedy of English education". (Central Press Photos Ltd.)

Back cover Elementary pupils at the St. George British School, Bristol, 1895. (Reece Winstone)

Early Victorian education:
Plate i Dr Guthrie's school for poor children in the early 1850s. (Mansell Collection)

The beginnings of popular education:
Plate ii (*top*) Life in the "British" monitorial school, devised by Joseph Lancaster: the factory-like schoolroom showing the "division of labour applied to intellectual purposes". With monitorial help, one master could control a thousand pupils. Note the curtains to divide the room, the pointers and reading sheets on the walls, and the reading circles marked on the floor. (From *British and Foreign School Society Manual* of 1816, by kind permission of the British and Foreign School Society)
(*centre and bottom*) Progressive infant teaching in the 1820s, from Samuel Wilderspin's *The Infant System*. The first picture shows the gallery that allowed "simultaneous activity", so that each child could see and contribute to an "object lesson". The lower picture shows children at spelling and reading lessons, grouped round lesson posts. (By permission of the Syndics of the University Library, Cambridge)

Nineteenth-century public school life:
Plate iii (*top*) Work in Lower School, Eton. (Radio Times Hulton)
(*bottom*) The public school boy, described in the Clarendon Report as "a high-spirited English lad, who has the restless activity and love of play that belong to youth and health … and to whom mental effort is troublesome". (Radio Times Hulton)

vi

Early Victorian girls' education:

Plate iv (*top*)   Family education at home: Papa conducts a geography lesson for four daughters and one son. (Gernsheim Collection, Humanities Research Center, The University of Texas at Austin)

(*bottom*)   The pioneer girls' high school, the North London Collegiate, in 1851, with girls gathered for Prize Day. (By kind permission of the Headmistress, North London Collegiate School)

Elementary education:

Plate v (*top*)   A *Punch* cartoon, commenting on the clash of religious and secular interests that destroyed several education Bills in the 1850s. (By kind permission of *Punch*)

(*bottom*)   The schoolchildren of the 1860s: Kelvedon British School, Essex. (By kind permission of Essex County Record Office)

Plate vi (*top*)   Concern for poor, homeless city children was one motive behind the 1870 Education Act. This *Graphic* drawing is entitled "The School or Gaol?" and captioned: "The wastefulness illustrated in the picture is so striking. If this heap of living creatures and of possible men be suffered to perish ... a something worth preserving, which we can never wholly replace, will perish with them." (The *Graphic*, December 24th 1870)

(*bottom*)   W. E. Forster and the 1870 Act, a clever compromise won from competing religious and political interests. In this cartoon by Tenniel, clergy and politicians fight amongst themselves, forgetting the ball, Education. The caption read: Mr. F-st-r (Umpire): "Boys, boys, this is fighting and not fair play! You've lost sight of the ball!" (By kind permission of *Punch*)

Plate vii   Hostility to the Board schools: Conservative resentment of their success and rising costs is seen in this cartoon of 1883, entitled "Education's Frankenstein". According to this viewpoint, if everyone is highly educated many will be unemployed. (Mansell Collection)

The growth of secondary education:

Plate viii (*top*)   Boys of Richmond Grammar School, Yorkshire, in 1868. (Radio Times Hulton)

(*bottom*)   A chemistry lesson at the Queen's Walk Higher Grade School, Nottingham. Ratepayers protested about the lavish equipment in the school. (By kind permission of B. H. Tolley, Nottingham University)

Plate ix (*top*)   A study scene at Haileybury in the late 1890s. Note the map of the South African wars on the wall. (By kind permission of The Master, Haileybury School)

(*bottom*)   Haileybury boys contemplate the school's memorial to the victims of the Imperial wars of the late Victorian era. Service in the Empire became an ambition for boys from public schools. (By kind permission of The Master, Haileybury School)

Experiment in independent schools:

Plate x (*top*) Boys at Abbotsholme progressive school, Derbyshire, sharing in the hay harvest. This was, according to the founder Cecil Reddie, a lesson to show the "link between God and Nature". Note the special "rational dress" clothes of the pupils. (By kind permission of the Headmaster, Abbotsholme School)

(*bottom*) Direct-method French and Latin teaching, using recordings, at the Perse School, Cambridge, about 1910. (By kind permission of the Headmaster, the Perse School)

Progress in girls' education:

Plate xi (*top*) A symbolic tug-of-war at the North London Collegiate School, 1889. To answer the question "Should girls wear stays?" sixteen non-corset wearers challenged "any able-bodied girls of the opposite persuasion to a trial of strength". The corsets lost the day. (By kind permission of the Headmistress, North London Collegiate School)

(*bottom*) Varying fashions among High School girls, a new social phenomenon in the streets of Edwardian London. (Mansell Collection)

Rural schools at the beginning of the twentieth century:

Plate xii Life in the rural school: these classroom views of Oxfordshire schools were taken as part of the county survey following the 1902 Act. Note the wall-charts, the lamps and, in the top picture, the old gallery for infants. (By kind permission of the Chief Education Officer, Oxfordshire)

Discipline and patriotism in the Edwardian elementary school:

Plate xiii (*top*) Large classes and rigid order at Ramsey School, Hunts. (By kind permission of Cambridgeshire Public Libraries)

(*bottom*) Saluting the flag: Empire Day, 1914, at Ben Jonson's School, London. (The *Sphere*, May 30th 1914. By kind permission of the City of Bradford Central Library)

Progressive ideas in education between the wars:

Plate xiv (*top*) A very early experiment in schools broadcasting, Elstow School, Bedfordshire, 1926. (BBC Copyright)

(*bottom*) Rural skills, including bee-keeping, being taught at Impington Village College, Cambridge, 1939. (By kind permission of the Warden, Impington Village College)

Schooling and the Second World War:

Plate xv (*top*) Schoolgirls, in uniform cloaks and gas masks, hurry to the air-raid shelters. Lessons might continue there during a raid. (Radio Times Hulton) (*bottom*) A war poster by Abram Games, 1942, showing the features of English life that the country was fighting to preserve. Here the new Village College building at Impington is used to reflect current ambitions to improve education. (Imperial War Museum)

Controversy about secondary education in post-war Britain:

Plate xvi (*top*) Highly academic education at England's leading grammar school, Manchester Grammar School, 1954. (Radio Times Hulton)
(*bottom*) Secondary schoolgirls of a new era at Kidbrooke Comprehensive School (1955), the first such large, purpose-built school in London. (Radio Times Hulton)

Prologue: English schooling before 1750

In medieval England, education grew up as part of the work of the Christian Church. The oldest English schools were formed in the shadow of the great cathedrals or were linked to large churches or monasteries in important towns. These "grammar schools" taught aspiring clerics to speak and read Latin—the language of the Christian religion, of scholarship, of law and government, and the "foundation, gate and source" of the seven "liberal arts" that made up medieval learning. A knowledge of Latin did not merely prepare a youth for a career in the church. It opened the door to other professions in diplomacy and administration.

The pupils of such schools were "youths endowed with the light and sharpness of ability", probably of middle-class origin, as only their families could afford the fees. Other feudal classes—knights and peasants—had their own education. A nobleman's son was reared in another noble house, where he learned fighting and hunting skills, and the etiquette of chivalry. His sister might be trained to read, sing, embroider, and run a household, either at home or in a convent. The peasant boy picked up his farming skills in childhood work. For the town boy, craft and trade guilds provided their own technical training through apprenticeships.

In the later Middle Ages it became fashionable for laymen to found schools by an "endowment", a grant of money or land. Chantry schools were common: the founder appointed a priest to say mass for his soul, and to teach deserving local boys. Wealthier patrons provided a building, or made their schools free to "poor" scholars.

Outstanding among these lay foundations were Winchester (1382) and Eton (1440). Both were independent colleges, endowed on a grand scale. At Winchester, founded by the rich local bishop, William of Wykeham, who rose to be Chancellor of England, seventy carefully chosen, non-local "poor and needy scholars" were to be boarded. Ten places were also found for "sons of noble and powerful persons". Eton, founded by Henry VI in 1440, deliberately aimed, with its splendid buildings, to excel its rival and "to be called the Lady Mother and Mistress of all other grammar schools".

These great foundations inspired many imitations on a lesser scale in the fifteenth century. Hundreds of endowments, large and small, covered the country with a network of schools.

Learning began in the "petty school", which taught reading to young children (including girls), aged from seven onwards, who were known as "ABCDarians". The alphabet was learned from a wooden tablet, the "hornbook". It began with the "cross row" (a cross was written before the letters ABC on the first reading line) and ended "Amen". The pupil then advanced to the "primer", a simple book of prayers and texts. Some elementary schools merely taught song, the hymns and psalms of divine service.

Age of entry to the grammar school—between nine and twelve—depended on a boy's progress with his "petite lernynge". Hours were long, continuing from dawn to dusk, the tedious day relieved only by prayers and rough meals. Each boy had his penner (sheaf of quill feathers), pen knife, inkhorn and candles. As classes were large to swell the master's income, discipline was maintained by relentless beating with the birch. A few written fragments survive to express the boys' hatred of school and their "fere of betynge". In the sixteenth century commonplace book of a London grocer, there is one rhyme in which a boy imagines hunting his master:

> I would my master were an hare
> And all his bokes howndes were
> And I myself a joly hontere;
> To blow my horn I wold not spare,
> For if he were dede I wold not care.

Teaching was oral in question-and-answer style, as books were rare until the fifteenth century. Latin was learned parrot fashion from grammarians, such as the Roman, Donatus. Older boys might study practical aspects of Latin: "dictamen"—the composition of business letters—or other forms of writing, such as drafting deeds or keeping legal records.

2

Medieval schools mostly remained in continuous session, with holidays on the great church festivals. There were two particular school feasts: St. Nicholas' Day, when a boy bishop was chosen in all great churches to preach a sermon, and Shrove Tuesday, marked by violent sports such as cock-fighting and crude football.

The upheaval of the English Reformation, brought about by Henry VIII and his son, Edward VI, in the 1530s and '40s, closed many schools, especially those connected to chantries, dissolved by an Act of 1547. Henry used some of the wealth confiscated from the monasteries to open "King's Schools", linked to the bishoprics of the reformed English Church. Scholars, churchmen and local worthies were able to persuade Edward VI to re-establish grammar schools, seeing them as the foundation of Protestant religion, and social stability and prosperity.

A pattern for these foundations was provided by St. Paul's in London, (1518). Here boys were to study in a style coloured by the Renaissance: they learned Greek as well as classical Latin, instead of Medieval Latin, "that filthiness ... which the later blind world brought in". Book learning replaced oral teaching. Lily's Latin grammar books were prescribed as standard texts in all schools by Henry VIII himself. English books, too—the Bible, Prayer Book, the King's Primer—began to influence the curriculum. Humanist writers suggested more enlightened teaching methods. Sir Thomas Elyot's *The Governour* (1531) deplored the "Grammar Grind", suggesting that boys be led by a "gentle old master" to understand the content of classical books. Roger Ascham, in *The Scholemaster* (1570) considered school should be "a house of play and pleasure", not of "fear and bondage", and protested against the cult of corporal punishment.

The many endowments by private benefactors during the reigns of Elizabeth I and James I produced a Golden Age of the grammar school. By 1600 there was one, it is claimed, within walking distance of any deserving boy. The intake was notable for social balance, tradesmen's sons mixing with those of gentlemen.

The early seventeenth century also produced many elementary or "English" schools, modestly endowed by some local patron, sometimes with a small school-house, or run by a clergyman in part of the village church. Here pupils learned to read, and perhaps write, English.

The Civil War of the 1640s did not seriously disrupt schools though some "malignant" Royalist schoolmasters were dismissed. Cromwell's republican government was ready to help institutions in financial difficulty. The Commonwealth period was notable for its radical educational discussion. Outstanding in the flood of reforming pamphlets was that by the poet, John Milton. His *Tractate of Education* (1644) best caught the spirit of the time: "The reforming of education ... be one of the greatest and noblest designs that can be thought on and for the want whereof this nation perishes."

The ambitious plans for universal education advanced by the widely-read Czech thinker, John Comenius, were much admired. The boldest of these English Comenians demanded compulsory, free state education for all. A pamphlet of 1659 visualized an "English" elementary school in every parish, with a grammar school in each town. No child should be neglected "for hereby hath it come to pass that many are now holding the plough, which might have been fit to steer the state".

The classical curriculum was also condemned, as "a show of knowledge like a parrot who speaks words but he knows not what he saith". Useful learning, for "the relief of man's estate", in the spirit of the dawning age of scientific enquiry, was advocated. Harsh discipline was deplored. A teacher, George Snell, protested that "slavish correction with the whip breedeth in the corrected ... a very hatred against the school, the teacher and against learning."

The plans and projects of the Commonwealth era ended in the reaction of Charles II's Restoration in 1660. The aristocracy and the Anglican Church, conservative and embittered, were also restored. This establishment saw education as partly responsible for the recent troubles. "The Bible under every weaver and chambermaid's arm hath done us much hurt", claimed the Earl of Newcastle. "But that which hath done us most hurt is the abundance of grammar schools." They had been educating boys out of their proper social station. "Those whom nature or fortune had determined to the plough, the oar, or other handicrafts, were being diverted to the study of Liberal Arts." So began the long decline of the grammar schools, that lasted into the eighteenth century. There were fewer foundations and fewer pupils.

Moreover, the Act of Uniformity of 1662 opened the great divide of Church and Chapel in English society. Not only clergymen but teachers too were now to conform to the Church of England's liturgy. Non-conformists became inferior citizens, isolated and persecuted. Barred from other outlets, they took successfully to business. Forbidden to teach, they defied the law by forming their own schools. Most of these were quite small, with a dozen boys gathered in a private house, ready to move quickly if authority investigated. Some of their pupils—Daniel Defoe, Isaac Watts, Samuel Wesley—became leading figures of their time. After the Toleration Act of 1689, penalties against non-conformists were relaxed, and their schools grew to be the most vital sector of English education in the eighteenth century. The Dissenting Academies were their finest achievement. These were almost universities, intended to train ministers. However, a broad curriculum allowed older boys to study "realistic" subjects, and the Academies contributed to the rise of science. The eminent scientist, Joseph Priestley, studied at Daventry and taught at Warrington Academy.

For centuries, education had barely affected the children of the poor. In 1726, the writer Jonathan Swift had summed up an age-long attitude: "The cottagers and labourers keep their children at home, their business being only to till and cultivate the earth, and therefore their education is of little consequence to the public." Chance for even the humblest kind of schooling at crude private or dame schools was limited and haphazard. Yet the eighteenth century was remarkable for the charity school movement that tried to provide large-scale educational opportunity for the very poorest of children.

The Society for Promoting Christian Knowledge (S.P.C.K.), founded in 1698, encouraged local bodies to found and collect funds for parochial elementary schools. The middle-class philanthropy, which subscribed to these schools, was inspired partly by Christian charity, partly by fear of the lower orders. A contemporary described the orphans and foundlings in the towns: "the little dirty infantry which swarms up and down the alleys and lanes with curses and ribaldry ... as if they intended to put off their humanity and degenerate into brutes." A circular of 1705 noted this mixture of motives behind the charity school: "A Christian and useful education of the children of the poor is absolutely necessary to their piety, virtue and honest livelihood ... also to the ease and security of all other people whatsoever."

There were the large hospitals (boarding schools) for city orphans, like the Greycoat Hospital in Westminster (1706) or Liverpool's Bluecoat School (1708) founded to relieve "the great misery that the poor children do generally suffer ... They become the curse and trouble of all places where they live." Children were housed and fed in impressive buildings. Country schools were small and plain, sometimes linked with almshouses. Many children had distinctive uniforms: there were blue, green, grey, orange, even yellow coat schools.

While the catechism of the Church of England formed the heart of the schools' curriculum, children were also taught to be "dutiful and obedient", learning their humble place in the social order, and to endure a life of poverty. All learned to read. Practical skills were taught, as "habits of industry" were highly valued as an antidote to social disorder.

The annual charity sermon in the local church supported weekly appeals for funds, a statue of the charity child being placed beside the collecting box. Children were paraded on Sundays, so that the middle classes might see living proof of their charitable works. A yearly service gathered thousands of children at St. Paul's Cathedral. This, commented the writer Joseph Addison was: "The glory of the age we live in ... such a numerous and innocent multitude, clothed in the charity of their benefactors, was a spectacle pleasing both to God and Man ... it seems to promise us an honest and virtuous posterity."

Such propaganda disguised the poor quality of many teachers, who ill-treated and exploited their pupils. Political and religious quarrels broke out among their administrators. Individual critics, like Bernard Mandeville, in *Charity and Charity Schools* (1724), expressed upper-class fears about the whole principle of the movement. Children would be spoiled by the softness of school life: "The more a shepherd, a ploughman or any other peasant knows of the world, the less fit he will be to go through the fatigues and hardships of it with cheerfulness and content." He concluded: "To make society happy and people easy under the meanest circumstances, it is requisite that great numbers of them should be ignorant as well as poor." Faith in the charity schools waned. By 1750, the movement was in decline.

1   Schooling for the poor: 1750–1865

In the eighteenth century, rigid class distinctions divided England. Society, it was thought, was a divinely-ordered mechanism in which everybody knew his place. The upper and middle classes, anxious to maintain established order, had two theories about the education of the poor. The first considered such schooling would be dangerous. A historian, George Hadley, writing in 1788, feared that reading would distract workers from toil: "What ploughman, who could read the renowned history of Tom Hickathrift, Jack the Giant-Killer, or The Seven Wise Men [characters in famous chap-books] would be content to whistle up one furrow and down another, from dawn in the morning, to the setting of the sun?" The horrors of the French Revolution (1789) only confirmed prejudice against widespread literacy. Reading of political and religious pamphlets would ferment disorder. "It is safest for both the Government and the religion of the country to let the lower classes remain in that state of ignorance in which nature has originally placed them," commented the Bishop of London in 1803.

The second theory held that simple schooling was a benefit, allowing the poor to read the Scriptures and to earn a useful, if humble, living, while learning gratitude to their social betters. The popular author, Hannah More, wrote in a tract of 1795: "I think to teach good principles to the lower classes is the most likely way to save the country. Now, in order to do this we must teach them to read."

Private enterprise schools

Where there was no charity school, a poor child's opportunity for schooling was limited. The vicar or parish clerk might teach children in some part of the village church, as graffiti and damaged monuments bear witness. Otherwise private enterprise supplied some chances. Anyone might set up a "school" and try to live by charging small fees (in contrast to the charity school-teacher who had an annual salary). The quality of such teachers varied greatly: they were united only by the low public esteem in which their work was held. Surviving diaries describe the teachers' work. Some were itinerant, instructing children and adults alike. Others were static, supplementing their fees by doing other useful work around the village: collecting rates, drawing up legal documents, reading the newspaper aloud, measuring fields. Memoirs of early working-class leaders recall the benefits conferred by a good teacher, a "kind religious man, loving and preserving order". Too many were "the refuse of society at large". Anyone reduced by misfortune might teach—a wounded soldier, a cripple or a failed tradesman. They were ignorant: a notice outside a Cambridgeshire school promised "reding, riting and gramer". They were sometimes dissolute. The drunkenness of the teacher was "almost proverbial". They were often cruel, sadly tormenting their pupils. The writer, Charles Lamb, recalled the beating ruler of his master, "with a delectable hole ... to raise blisters, like a cupping glass".

Dame schools remained common until the 1850s. An elderly woman took children into her cottage, taught knitting and "half-taught" them to read, still using the age-old hornbook with the "cross row". All the equipment needed, it was said, was a notice saying "Children taught to read and work here", a rod to beat them and a corner in which to stand the dunce. Sentimental portraits of dames abound. The Chartist, Thomas Cooper, described his dame as "an expert and laborious teacher ... I soon became her favourite scholar and could read the tenth Chapter of Nehemiah, with all its hard names, 'like the parson in church', as she used to say ..." The grim, fictitious portrait of the poverty of the teacher, Ellen Orford, in George Crabbe's poem, *The Borough* (1810), probably reflects a common reality.

After 1760, what the historian G. M. Trevelyan called "the long era of content", came to an end. English life was rapidly changed, firstly by enclosure in the countryside, by which the labourer lost his common land and therefore his life of semi-independence, and secondly by mechanical manufacturing processes which made the Industrial Revolution. In the mushroom towns that grew round factories and mills, the problem of the poor and their children grew more complex and alarming.

The value of child labour to work the new machines was quickly exploited. Demand for child workers soon exceeded supply. Parish workhouses were ransacked for children, who were carted off to the sparsely-populated manufacturing districts. The mill-owners were described as "a species of slave proprietor".

While children could prove so profitable, schemes for popular education were less favourably received. In this climate, the "School of Industry" became a common device for poor relief. Pauper children were taught a skill and their produce sold to support the school. Thus, at a school in Fincham (Norfolk), sixty children plaited straw; at Chester, four schools—to which girls went in rotation—taught knitting, spinning, sewing and washing. Such successes encouraged even highest authority to see them as a social benefit. Prime Minister Pitt's scheme for Poor Law Reform (1796) envisaged industrial schools for all children of parents receiving poor relief. However, competition from factories undermined the schools. Their pupils became "puny and weak" from overwork and "extremely ignorant" of anything except their particular craft.

One phenomenon of the factory age was the "stirring of dry bones" within the Church, following the challenge of Methodism. The Sunday School movement reflected this revival. The Gloucester business man and journalist, Robert Raikes (1735–1811) became its spokesman. In 1780 he became worried about children working in the city's chief industry, pin making. On Sundays, they ran wild "cursing and swearing in a manner so horrid as to convey to any serious mind an idea of hell rather than any other place". Raikes hired some "decent, well disposed women" to teach them. Local clergymen took up the idea, which was soon successful. In 1784 Raikes reported: "A woman who lives in a lane where I had fixed a school told me ... that the place was quite a heaven upon Sundays compared to what it used to be." Parents and employers were enthusiastic as the schools were cheap and run outside working hours; children were bribed by presents. John Wesley's Journal of 1784 noted: "I find these schools springing up wherever I go." They were the beginning of real popular education.

The long school day alternated instruction in reading and the Catechism with church services, aiming to inspire in pupils "good and industrious behaviour in their future character of labourers and

9

servants." Titles from the library of a Newcastle school catch the flavour of the work: *Precious Remedies for Satan's Devices* or *Sighs from Hell*. Punishment could be fierce, blocks of wood being tied to truants' feet. Raikes himself was known to press the fingers of a boy liar onto a hot stove. Teachers were voluntary workers, "persons of superior abilities or rank" being preferred.

Although cynics protested against "converting Sunday into a schoolday", the Sunday schools were valuable. For example, Hannah More's twelve schools in the Mendips brought a civilizing spirit to a rough district: "Warrants for wood stealing, pilfering etc. are quite out of fashion." Secondly, they taught young and old to read. Evening classes even taught the elderly. Dr. Poole, historian of the movement, described how "many acknowledged with tears of gratitude and joy flowing down their furrowed cheeks the greatness of the blessing conferred upon them." Fortunes were made by publishers selling chap-books or moralistic readers to this wider reading public.

The success of the Sunday schools aroused interest in a national system of day schools. The problems of cost, child numbers and lack of teachers were tackled by the monitorial school, which became a fashion in the early nineteenth century.

By the monitorial principle, the master instructed older, abler pupils who then passed on their lessons to younger school-fellows. It was not new: medieval Winchester, the seventeenth century grammar school, even the Sunday school, had used the method. However, the famous practitioners, Joseph Lancaster (1778–1838) and Andrew Bell (1753–1832) used it on so large a scale that it seemed a fresh discovery.

Bell, a Scottish clergyman, had run an orphan school for soldiers' children in Madras, India. When his staff refused to use Indian sand trays to teach writing, he appointed boys to teach their classes, with great success. In 1797, Bell published *An Experiment in Education*, claiming that one master, with monitor assistants, could teach twenty times the number of pupils that he could teach working alone. He tried his "Madras system" in various English schools where it "worked like magic ... order and regularity started up all at once."

Lancaster, a Quaker, had started a free school for the poor in Southwark in 1798. His genius as a teacher won him hundreds of pupils. To save the cost of assistants, he used monitors to teach younger children. By 1805 he had over eight hundred pupils. His results were described in *Improvements in Education* (1803). His Borough Road school drew important visitors: "Foreign princes, ambassadors, peers, commoners, ladies of distinction, bishops and archbishops, all visited it with wonder-waiting eyes", commented Lancaster's biographer. In 1805, King George III bestowed royal patronage on the idea, announcing: "It is my wish that every poor child in my dominions shall be taught to read the Bible."

The monitorial system was admired for its cheapness and its ability to handle large numbers. It seemed, too, to fit the age of the factory. It was, wrote an admirer, "worthy to stand ... parallel and rival to the most useful modern inventions". The poet Coleridge described it as "an incomparable machine", a "vast, moral steam engine".

The systems of Bell and Lancaster used the same principles yet differed in detail. Bell's was easier for others to imitate, as Lancaster was obsessed with minute points. Lessons were carefully organized with all tasks subdivided into simple elements, so that the complex hierarchy of monitors—each with his particular task—could easily understand their work. Everything was taught mechanically; everyone was ceaselessly busy. "Method, order, regulation," wrote Bell. "It is in school as in the army: discipline is the first, second and third essential."

Lancaster valued motivation highly, and devised elaborate rewards and punishments. Top boys in each reading group received a leather badge or small picture, while kites, hoops and rackets hung from roof beams as prospective prizes. Excellent pupils received silver medals, and a herald proclaimed their merits at prize day. By contrast, there were cruel punishments designed to humiliate offenders: they might be shackled together, tied to their desks, or hung from the roof in baskets "in the sight of all the pupils, who frequently smile at the birds in the cage". They might be labelled with their fault. Dirty boys were publicly washed by girls.

The two pioneers met and corresponded, and borrowed each other's ideas. In 1805, Mrs. Trimmer, a school-book writer, claimed that Lancaster had stolen his system from Bell. Moreover, his non-conformity made him a dangerous influence. Others followed in attacking Lancaster, as "the Goliath of schismatics", whose work could bring "general infidelity". A debate began that split national opinion.

From this quarrel sprang factions whose arguments were to hinder educational progress until 1870. Societies were formed. Lancaster's Quaker friends, disturbed by his extravagance, formed the Royal Lancasterian Society in 1808, which became the British and Foreign School Society in 1814. William Allen, a Quaker philanthropist, took the title literally in spreading the "British School" system at home and abroad in Europe and the colonies. Lancaster, who resigned his interest, departed for America where he died penniless.

Church of England supporters founded The National Society for the Education of the Poor in 1811. There was a model school in London and a training centre where "the beautiful and efficient simplicity of the system" was taught. The old charity schools, even some decayed grammar schools, were taken over. By 1813, the Society had 230 schools and 40,000 scholars. Dr. Bell won promotion and wealth. His satisfaction with his "invention" continued; to a friend he wrote: "We shall see this system of tuition spread over the world."

Monitorial teaching was copied in private and grammar schools. In 1817 it also spread to Charterhouse, the famous public school, where it was used briefly to teach classics. It became a fashionable craze in family tuition. Yet it eventually disappointed its supporters. Its weakness lay in the use of child teachers who were, noted a critic, "little more than infants, without training ... (who) were set to waste their own time and that of their still younger companions under the nominal supervision of a teacher." While the competition of the two societies spread popular schooling, the mass methods and cheapness of the monitorial school debased the ideal of education.

State intervention in elementary schooling

The idea that the state should help provide education was only accepted gradually in nineteenth century England. Other European countries, coloured by Napoleon's influence, had begun state systems: Holland with elementary education (1808); France (1806) and Prussia (1810) with High Schools and Universities. England, at war with Napoleon and resisting the very notion of his kind of state, favoured the philosophy of *laissez-faire*, that is, that government should not interfere in individual action. Mechanisms of state control, at national and local level, were only developed reluctantly. The Church clung stubbornly to its traditional monopoly, in support of the parent's "sacred duty" to care for his child. Church leaders considered voluntary effort enough to provide the schooling that was required. Employers (anxious to retain their child workers) cynically commended the "sacred obligations" of labour. Education, said a spokesman, would rear "an effeminate class of persons, averse to rough work, conceited and insubordinate". By contrast, reformers who exposed the horrors of child labour and crime claimed it was a nation's duty to care for its young. Slowly, as voluntary funds could not cope with such a massive problem, government became involved in the financing and administration of popular education.

Enclosure and industrialization brought widespread unemployment. By 1803 a ninth of the population were receiving poor relief. The condition of their children worried reformers. In 1807 the philanthropist, Samuel Whitbread, proposed a Poor Law Bill in which a key place was given to education, that "panacea [universal remedy] for the ills to which our state was naturally subjected." Whitbread hoped that a system of parochial elementary schools, like that lately adopted in Scotland, would reduce crime and pauperism, and "exalt the character of the labourer". The Bill was defeated, mostly by the Bishops who disliked the proposal that democratic committees should run the Schools. "The first principle of education in this country", said the Archbishop of Canterbury, was that it should be "under the control and auspices of the Establishment."

The slump after the Napoleonic Wars in 1815 did not produce conditions favourable to educational progress. Popular demands for reform of all kinds were sternly repressed. Yet the lawyer Henry Brougham (1778–1868), inspired by radicals (left-wing thinkers) who saw literacy as a preparation for working-class political power, persuaded Parliament to inquire into "The Education of the Lower Orders" in 1816. The Committee's statistics showed that only one child in sixteen attended school. Brougham condemned England as "the worst educated country of Europe". He then turned his attention to the old educational endowments, and found so much dishonesty in their application that "the intention of the donor seems entirely perverted". He suggested, vainly, that the funds should be redeployed to provide schools for the poor. His Parochial Schools Bill of 1820 was rejected.

In the late 1820s the old Tory social order crumbled. The repeal of the Test Acts (1828) allowed non-conformists a larger influence in the nation's affairs. The Reform Act (1832) gave the franchise to the middle classes, the "New Men" who had made industrial fortunes.

The question of educational reform could now be re-considered. Petitions flowed into the reformed Parliament. Another champion, J. A. Roebuck, proposed that "the House proceed to devise means for the universal and national education of the whole people." Taking the recently devised Irish Education Board as a model, Roebuck suggested compulsory schooling for all. The country would be divided into school districts, each under a committee, all overseen by a Minister of Public Instruction. Such action would create a people "industrious, honest, tolerant and happy".

His plan was too ambitious, yet government interest was sufficient to allow a grant of £20,000 to be made to help school-building by the National and British Societies. This modest act of 1833 was a historic turning point: the first practical act involving the state in England's schooling.

Pressure for further intervention grew. Detailed surveys, such as those of the Manchester Statistical Society, showed that many children were untouched by education. By 1836 a Central Society of Education was demanding a government authority to found schools, train teachers and supervise grants. At last, in 1839, a Committee of the Privy Council was appointed to consider "all matters affecting the education of the people". Its first Secretary was the remarkable Dr. James Kay-Shuttleworth (1804–77).

He had been a Manchester doctor, who had exposed the condition of the slums in widely-read reports. Thereafter he had become an Assistant Commissioner for the New Poor Law of 1834, first in East Anglia, then in London. At the industrial school attached to the Norwood Union Workhouse he found children "covered only with rags and vermin", existing in "mental darkness". He applied ideas taken from European reformers whose work he went to see for himself. As a result, the school day became "a cheerful succession of instruction, recreation, work and domestic and religious duties". Children of "malign aspect" and "stubborn temper" began to "display in their features evidence of happiness". This work earned him his post on the Committee of Council.

Kay-Shuttleworth needed diplomatic skill in his work. The Oxford Movement of 1833 onwards had revived the Church of England. The "religious difficulty" in education debate sharpened, as extremists joined in. Archdeacon Denison, for example, thought no "National" school should be open to a dissenter's child. By contrast, a non-conformist Voluntaryist party was formed led by the journalist, Edward Baines, to oppose state interference in "British" schools. These "secularists" followed the philosopher Jeremy Bentham, who considered education as an individual right and social duty. They ridiculed church-school teaching: biblical sums ("our Lord showed himself to the Apostles forty days after his passion. For how many weeks was he not seen?") or religious alphabets:

> A is an Angel, who praises the Lord;
> B is for Bible, God's most holy word;
> C is for Church, where the righteous resort;
> D is for Devil who wishes our hurt.

The great Victorian thinkers and reformers—John Stuart Mill, Dickens, Carlyle—lent their mighty support to this side of the debate.

The condition of working children was made terribly clear by a series of reports on factories, mines and agriculture that shocked the national conscience. The 1842 Report on children in mining disturbed most: five-year-olds stood in water and darkness all day working ventilation doors; boys and girls dragged carts of coal underground "harnessed like dogs in a go-cart". An 1843 Report described gangs of children, hired from contractors to work East Anglian farms, exposed to long hours and all weathers. Thomas Carlyle in *Past and Present* (1843) expressed the horror that swept England: "The working body of this rich English nation has sunk into a state to which there is literally no parallel."

A series of Factory Acts earlier in the century had tried to limit exploitation of children in various trades. In 1843 a more ambitious Factory Bill was proposed by Sir James Graham, the Home Secretary: state-built, church-run factory schools should give child workers some education. Because of non-conformist opposition, only a fragment of the scheme passed. "Half-timer" working children were to produce a certificate for Inspectors, showing part-time attendance at some school. The scheme was never satisfactory, although it lingered until 1918. Exhausted "half-timers" mixed uneasily with full-time pupils. "In the clothing districts", reported an Inspector, "their faces, necks and hands are deeply stained with the blue of the dye—from the spinning mills they come covered with the 'flock of the yarn'—their hair thickly powdered with it ..."

While the government could not act, private enterprise again stepped in. Remarkable in the 1840s was the Ragged School Union, which opened schools in the slums of great cities, supported by the reformer, the Earl of Shaftesbury. Volunteer teachers sought vagrant children, "the shoeless, shirtless and capless" and tried "to convert incipient criminals to Christianity". Charles Dickens described a Holborn Ragged School "held in a low-roofed den in a sickening atmosphere ... The pupils sang, fought, danced, robbed each other—seemed possessed by legions of devils ... The lights were blown out and the books strewn in the gutters." Later schools were better ordered with paid teachers. There were two hundred such schools by 1869.

Kay-Shuttleworth worked steadily through the 1840s to extend the range of government activity in education, to improve existing schools and to limit "the ignorance, nay barbarism" of English youth.

The Committee's first act was to appoint Inspectors. Kay-Shuttleworth took the Dutch inspectorate as his model, which was not "a means of exercising control but of affording assistance". His men were to diffuse new ideas through the schools and to educate public opinion. Her Majesty's Inspectors (H.M.I.s) laboriously travelled their districts, filling in minutely-detailed forms and commenting thoughtfully on what they saw. Giant among them was Matthew Arnold (1822–88), son of Thomas Arnold, the Headmaster of Rugby School. As well as being a distinguished poet and writer, Matthew Arnold was an H.M.I. for thirty-five years from 1851.

Bad buildings and poor teachers are the themes of the first Inspectors' reports. Schools were held in leaking hovels, attics, parts of churches. In a Welsh school one Inspector described the "hot sickening smell which struck me on opening the door of that low dark room ... it more nearly resembled the smell of the engine on board a steamer, such as is felt by a sea-sick voyager in passing near the funnel." At another, books were "mere fragments, consisting of a few soiled sheets". In many schools "silence was only maintained for a few moments at a time, by exclamation and threat."

To improve standards, the Committee's Minutes of 1840 began the control of school sites and buildings. By 1847 an album of designs by the architect, H. E. Kendall, established the model Victorian church school: "The styles of the Middle Ages are best suited for school houses ... because the buildings themselves partake

... of a semi-religious character." Playgrounds and "galleries" on the Scottish model became popular. Single school-rooms persisted, although Kay-Shuttleworth favoured the curtain to divide groups.

Teacher training was the crucial part of Kay-Shuttleworth's reform. The monitorial system was now discredited. Monitors were, wrote an Inspector, "the unfittest of teachers ... they teach miserably." The teacher, with feeble monitorial help, struggled with large unruly classes. "He pauses in his discourse and listens", wrote another Inspector. "The perspiration begins to appear on his forehead, and a blow with his cane upon the map indicates the state of his feelings ..."

When his proposal for a state training college was rejected by the Church, Kay-Shuttleworth decided to found his own in Battersea. His inspiration was a Normal School he had seen in Switzerland; he had been charmed by "the union of ... intellectual attainment ... with the utmost simplicity of life". Peasant youths trained to teach their fellow poor, feeding themselves by their work in the fields. Kay-Shuttleworth remembered them singing traditional songs as they peeled home-grown vegetables for dinner. Battersea began with similar ideals. Youths trained for three years, working a spartan day of study and physical labour, with little recreation. Its founders hoped it would "plead its own cause with the government and the public". Although Battersea struggled financially and was handed to the National Society in 1843, it caused many imitations. By 1845, there were twenty-two training colleges scattered across the country. Their life was strenuous and austere. The curriculum, preparing for the official Teaching Certificate, was wide and pedantic. Dickens mocked the product of such courses in the teacher, McChoakumchild, in *Hard Times* (1854): "He and some one hundred and fifty other schoolmasters had been lately turned at the same time, in the same factory, like so many pianoforte legs. He had answered volumes of head-breaking questions ..."

In 1846, Kay-Shuttleworth introduced the pupil-teacher system, which he had used at Norwood. Good schools were to be bases for five-year apprenticeships for able thirteen-year-olds. Pupil-teachers received modest salaries; their instructors were given extra payment. At eighteen, the young people could compete for Queen's Scholarships, taken up at a training college. The scheme quickly succeeded. By 1849 an Inspector described the pupil-teachers as "a right-minded, well-behaved, intelligent and interesting class".

Others, however, soon noted that they were lacking in "animation and energy" after a long day with big classes, in a regime where scrubbing floors in school was considered "healthy bodily exercise".

When Kay-Shuttleworth retired in 1848, he had achieved much. The later pioneer, W. E. Forster, described him as "the man to whom ... we owe national education in England".

In the early 1850s Inspectors' reports were optimistic about progress. Public enthusiasm for education grew. Yet Bills proposing state schools where local provision was inadequate still foundered on religious jealousies. Rising hopes were blighted by the cost of the Crimean War (1854–6). In searching for economies, the government saw education grants as an obvious scapegoat: the £150,000 of 1851 had quadrupled by 1858. A Royal Commission, chaired by the Duke of Newcastle, was set up to inquire into "the present state of popular education in England" and to propose methods to extend "sound and cheap elementary instruction to all classes of the people".

The Newcastle Report (1851) concluded, from doubtful statistics, that "there are very few [poor children] who do not see the inside of something which may be called a school". The commissioners, touring selected town and country districts, found poor schools with "children, as closely packed as birds in a nest, and tumbling over each other like puppies in a kennel". Equipment was lacking: in one place "the chief text book seemed to be a kitten, to which all the children were very attentive". There were unsuitable teachers, "domestic servants out of place, discharged barmaids, vendors of toys or lollipops ... cripples almost bedridden." Yet the inspected schools, "the superiority of (which) may be stated as beyond dispute" gave hope, and trained teachers were "altogether a superior class to those who preceded them".

However, the Report noted a "lack of thorough grounding" in basic subjects. Schooling was too elaborate, aiming "not to make ploughboys or mechanics, but to make scholars". There should be "a searching examination ... of every child in every school to which grants are to be paid, with the view to ascertaining whether these elements of knowledge are thoroughly acquired."

This suggestion was swiftly accepted. In 1856, the Committee of Council had become the Education Department, with a Vice-President, a politician, who sat in Parliament. In 1859 this post was taken by Robert Lowe (1811-92). He openly despised democracy, believing that "the lower classes ought to be educated ... that they may appreciate and defer to higher motivation". His Permanent Secretary, R. Lingen, made himself hated by the "insolent, tyrannical and unwise" conduct of his office. These two devised a new Code of Regulations concerning school grants.

In 1862 this Revised Code was presented to Parliament. It aimed to save public money and to simplify the Department's administration. School managers were to receive the grants under a ruthless system of "payment by results". Pupils were to be arranged in six "standards": each could earn his school twelve shillings (60p) a year, if he passed the appropriate tests in reading, writing and arithmetic, and if he attended school regularly. The teacher's life, described by the Newcastle Report as "full of advantages at the public expense", was made more difficult, as his salary now depended on his pupils' results. Other grants, including those for pupil teachers and training colleges were cut.

Lowe defended his Code with typical bluntness: "We do not profess to give these children an education that will raise them above their station and business in life ... but to give them an education that may fit them for that business." His critics thought the code was "an act of spoliation ever to be remembered with shame". It swiftly changed the schools. Kay-Shuttleworth, writing in 1868, angrily described the decay of the pupil-teacher system, "the sinews of English public instruction", as the status and salaries of teachers fell. Matthew Arnold thought that "The mode of teaching in the primary schools has certainly fallen off. I find in them ... a deadness, a slackness and a discouragement." Yet, he noted grimly, the Code seemed a fair reflection of a society that valued culture less than "politics, business, money-making, pleasure ..." The teachers themselves recorded their chronic anxieties in the log-books they had to keep after 1863.

Lowe was driven from office in 1864, accused of interfering with Inspectors' reports. Yet the spirit of his Revised Code lived on in the elementary schools to the end of the century.

Experiment in elementary teaching

The century after 1750 saw some notable English experiments in the teaching of young children, following the ideas of some outstanding European educational thinkers.

Fundamental to these experiments was a new sympathy with the nature of the child. That was memorably expressed in a deeply influential book, *Émile*, by Jean Jacques Rousseau (1712–78). This described the education, "according to nature", of an imaginary boy. Rousseau thought the child grew in stages, each with "a perfection, a ripeness of its own". The child's learning activity should be appropriate for these stages. "Begin by making a careful study of your scholars", Rousseau advised the teacher. Adults were "always looking for the man in the child without considering what he is before he becomes a man."

Rousseau's followers often misunderstood his work. Some tried to follow his ideas literally, combining them with the concept of the "noble savage", whose simple, "natural" life had been described by Pacific explorers. The educational writer, David Williams, saw an English child reared in this "natural" way: he was thin, showing signs of "premature decay". He was illiterate and spoke only a jargon language. Thomas Day, author of a popular imitation of *Émile*, *Sandford and Merton* (1789), tried rearing two orphan girls to make himself a perfect wife. His favourite became a coquette. His friend Richard Edgeworth (1744–1817), father of eighteen children, reared his eldest son as a "child of nature", who merely turned disobedient. He did, however, produce a useful book, *Practical Education* (1798), which influenced home teaching. Even the extraordinary Brontë children were raised, in spartan "natural" style, according to "the ideas of Rousseau and Mr. Day".

More important in the everyday school world were other European educationists, who translated Rousseau's theories into practical form. Switzerland especially became a place of pilgrimage for progressive Englishmen, drawn to the school at Yverdun run by J. H. Pestalozzi (1746–1827).

Pestalozzi's theories about teaching young children were described in *How Gertrude teaches her Children* (1801). The heart of the work was a loving relationship, like that between mother and child. The teacher should then follow "nature's march of development", observing the stages of mental growth, working from the concrete to the abstract. "Head, hand and heart" should be developed together to make the whole man.

Among his followers was Robert Owen (1771–1858), a rich Manchester cotton trader and pioneer socialist. He had been horrified by Lancashire slums, and thought that a better environment could improve men's characters. When he bought the cotton mills at New Lanark in Scotland, he not only changed the factories but laid down rules for his workers' homes and behaviour: the community became "conspicuously honest, industrious, sober and orderly". Owen also provided schools, a Lancasterian monitorial model for older children, and a remarkable infant school, opened in 1816. Instruction began with devices to stimulate the senses: maps and brightly coloured pictures of animals hung on the walls; natural objects lay on the tables. Learning came from discussion, based on the children's curiosity. There was dancing and singing, and hand-clapping to numbers. The school followed "the plans prescribed in Nature". Its atmosphere was joyful. "The little creatures", wrote a visitor, "ran in groups to seize their benefactor by the hand, or to pull him by the coat, with the most artless simplicity." However, Owen's Quaker partners resented his "infidel views" on religion, and were worried by the dancing and drill. In 1824 the school was altered to a more austere regime. Its magic faded, and it eventually closed. Fifty years later, a follower of Owen, George Holyoake, visited the deserted school-room and found the remains of the canvas paintings "of immense dimension ... well and brightly painted", lying wrecked against the walls.

The English Infant School Movement also borrowed from Pestalozzi. In 1818, Henry Brougham started an Owenite infant school in London. A second school, opened in Spitalfields in 1820, was taught by Samuel Wilderspin (1792–1866), who became the English authority on the subject. He learned his craft the hard way. On the first morning of school, his homesick pupils pressed "in one dense mass, crying, yelling and kicking against the door", only to be silenced by a clothes prop, surmounted by a lady's cap, which Wilderspin waved to amuse them. "The charms of this wonderful instrument ... soon vanished and there would have been a sad relapse but for the marchings, gambols and antics I found it necessary to adopt." Thus he deduced his first principle: "That the great secret of training them was to descend to their level and become a child."

Wilderspin set out his experience in *The Infant System* (1852). As important as the school-room was the playground, the "uncovered school-room", vital for child growth, and useful for the teacher to observe: "If they play at what they choose, they are free beings and manifest their characters." Infants were taught through the senses, with special Wilderspin apparatus: coloured pictures, objects pinned to boards, brass letters, toy animals, counting frames. Wilderspin drew a large map of England on the floor and set children to walk out journeys by various routes. Moralistic chanted rhymes were used, as was music "to soften the feelings ... and improve the temper".

In 1824, an Infant School Society was founded. Wilderspin travelled the country in propaganda work. By 1825, thirty-five schools were open. On his journeys, Wilderspin met two Scottish pioneers, John Wood of Edinburgh and David Stow of Glasgow, whose ideas he added to his own.

Other disciples of Pestalozzi were less enlightened. Dr. Charles Mayo had been English Chaplain at Yverdun. In 1826 he opened his Cheam School, and later published books on infant schooling. He and his sister grossly misinterpreted Pestalozzi's ideas: the subtle gradations of his sense instruction became the dreary textbook, *Lessons on Objects* (1829). The object lesson, with its lists of difficult words, was to become a feature of elementary teaching. Wilderspin hated this "parrot system" that "fills the memory with useless rubbish". Such teaching was satirized by Dickens in *Hard Times* (1854) where a schoolboy defines a horse as a "graminivorous quadruped".

In contrast was the outstanding school at King's Somborne, Dorset, opened in 1842 by Richard Dawes (1793–1867). A keen scientist, Dawes trained children to observe and reason, relating his lessons to actual experience. His pupils calculated wind speed from cloud shadows; worked out water pressure on fish in streams; compared animals' teeth. Clubs were formed to carry on their projects. Children borrowed books to read to their parents, who found "new sources of happiness and of social comfort". Dawes became an authority on education, condemning the conventional National school as "a deception, retarding the cause of education rather than advancing it". Its instruction was "absolutely valueless".

Such pioneers showed ways forward that were eventually to become a characteristic part of English education.

Poor Reuben Dixon has the noisiest school
Of ragged lads who ever bow'd to rule;
Low is his price—the men who heave the coals
And clean our causeways send him boys in shoals.

    ... His labour praise deserves
But not our pity; Reuben has no nerves;
'Mid noise and dirt and stench and play and prate,
He calmly cuts the pen or views the slate.

GEORGE CRABBE
The Borough (1810)

The grand principle of Dr. Bell's system is the division of labour applied to intellectual purposes ... The principle in schools and manufactories is the same ...

SIR THOMAS BERNARD
The Education of the Poor (1809)

I can never forget the impression the scene made upon me. Here I beheld a thousand children collected from the streets, where they learned nothing but mischief ... all reduced to the most perfect order, and training to habits of subordination and usefulness, and learning the great truths of the Gospel.

WILLIAM ALLEN
Description of Lancaster's Borough Road School (1808)

Even vaccination, the most valuable discovery in the physical art, of which this country can boast, falls short of this invention; which provides the means of supplying a remedy for the disorders of filth, idleness, ignorance and vice, more fatal to children than the ravages of the small-pox.

ANDREW BELL
The Madras System (1808)

Giving education to the labouring classes of the poor ... would be prejudicial to their morals and happiness; it would teach them to despise their lot in life instead of making them good servants in agriculture and other laborious employments ... It would render them fractious and refractory ... it would enable them to read seditious pamphlets, vicious books and publications against Christianity; it would render them insolent to their superiors ...

DAVIES GIDDY M.P.
Commons debate on Whitbread's Bill (1807)

There have been periods when the country heard with dismay that "the soldier is abroad". That is not the case now ... There is another person abroad ... the schoolmaster is abroad—and I trust more to him, armed with his primer, than I do to the soldier in full military array, for upholding the labours of his country.

HENRY BROUGHAM
Commons speech (1828)

Future generations ... while enjoying all the blessings of an impartial and efficient system of public instruction, will find it difficult to believe that the authors of that system should have had to struggle with a vehement and pertinacious opposition, and that such an opposition was offered in the name of civil and religious freedom.

THOMAS MACAULAY
Commons Speech (1847)

If the whole English people be not educated ... a tremendous responsibility will rest somewhere—How dare any man ... stand up in any Parliament or place ... and for a day or an hour forbid God's light to come into the world and bid the Devil's darkness continue in it one hour more ...

THOMAS CARLYLE
Past and Present (1843)

The Creator, having breathed a mind into a person, must have intended him to be educated.

CHARLES DICKENS
Speech to a Mechanics' Institute (1847)

Is it not almost a self-evident axiom that the State should require and compel the education of every human being who is born a citizen?

JOHN STUART MILL
On Liberty (1859)

They come forth! The mine delivers its gang and the pit its bondsmen ... The plain is covered with the swarming multitude ... Troops of youths—Alas! of both sexes ... all are clad in male attire; and oaths that men might shudder at issue from lips born to breathe words of sweetness. Yet these are to be the Mothers of England! ... Naked to the waist, an iron chain fastened to a leather belt runs between their legs ... On hands and feet, an English girl, for twelve, sometimes sixteen hours a day, hauls and hurries tubs of coal up subterranean passages, dark, precipitous and plashy ...

BENJAMIN DISRAELI
Sybil (1845)

*To raise the character and position of the schoolmaster ... to render
the school popular among the poor, as a means of introducing their
children to more honourable and profitable employment, and ... to
create in the minds of the working class a juster estimate of the value
of education for their children.*

J. KAY-SHUTTLEWORTH
Aims of the pupil-teacher system, Minute (1846)

*We must make up our minds to see the last of him ... at 10 or 11. It is
quite possible to teach a child soundly and thoroughly ... all that it is
necessary for him to possess ... by the time he is 10 years old ... He
should be able to spell correctly ... he shall read a common
narrative—a paragraph in the newspaper ... he shall write his
mother a letter ... he knows enough of ciphering to make out ... a
common shop bill ... He has acquaintances enough with the Holy
Scriptures to follow the allusions and the arguments of a plain Saxon
sermon.*

REV. T. FRAZER
Limits for schooling of the poor, Newcastle Report (1861)

*I cannot promise the House that this system will be an economical one
and I cannot promise that it will be an efficient one, but I can promise
that it shall be either one or the other. If it is not cheap, it shall be
efficient: if it is not efficient, it shall be cheap.*

ROBERT LOWE
The Revised Code. Commons speech (1862)

*Nature wants children to be children before they are men. If we
deliberately pervert this order, we shall get premature fruits which
are neither ripe nor well flavoured and which soon decay ...
childhood has ways of seeing, thinking and feeling peculiar to itself:
nothing can be more foolish than to substitute our ways for theirs.*

JEAN JACQUES ROUSSEAU
Émile (1762)

*What is the true type of education? It is like the art of the gardener
under whose care a thousand trees blossom and grow. He contributes
nothing to their actual growth ... He plants and waters but God gives
the increase ... So with the educator: he imparts no simple power to
man ... He takes care that development runs its course in accordance
with its Laws.*

J. H. PESTALOZZI
Address to My House (1818)

2 Schooling for the upper and middle classes: 1780–1860

The rise of the public schools

Although many grammar schools were in decline at the end of the eighteenth century, a few were sufficiently large and attractive to the upper classes to become distinguished as the "Great Schools" or "Public Schools".

An élite of schools made up "The Seven". Winchester and Eton drew aristocratic, even royal, patronage. Westminster, an Elizabethan foundation, won esteem under the late seventeenth century Head, Richard Busby, who reared many great men of his time. Three others had been small local schools moulded by ambitious Headmasters. Harrow (1571) had been changed by a typical process: the "foreigners" (non-local, fee-paying boys) came to out-number local boys, forming a boarding school for sons of the wealthy. Shrewsbury (1552) had once been "The Eton of Wales and Shropshire". It was rescued from decay by an innovating Head, Samuel Butler, who forged its distinguished academic reputation after 1798. Rugby (1576) moved to a larger site with new buildings after 1780, after the sale of London land formerly owned by its founder, Lawrence Sheriff. Finally there was Charterhouse (1611) founded for sons "of impoverished gentlemen ... soldiers who had borne arms by land or sea, merchants, and servants of the King and Queen".

Three other schools were sometimes placed beside "The Seven". Two day-schools, St. Paul's and Merchant Taylors, were highly regarded, as was the charitable foundation, Christ's Hospital, which still dressed its scholars in Elizabethan blue coat and yellow stockings. "The tradesmen and householders of London look with an eye of peculiar affection on the Blue-coat boy as he passes along the streets", wrote the poet, Samuel Coleridge, of his old school.

Although the definition of a "public school" remained elusive, the schools shared certain features: their independence, long history, conservatism, close ties with Oxford and Cambridge, and their Latin and Greek curriculum. They considered themselves "the guardians of the old tradition".

Comment on the schools in the early nineteenth century tended to polarize: they provoked either sentimental praise or bitter criticism. The classical curriculum was a centre of controversy. Masters taught Latin and Greek because they were the traditional work of the school. Arguments had also been invented to justify them. They were difficult, therefore they were educative. Latin was "absolutely necessary to a gentleman", no speech in the House of Commons being complete without its classical quotations. The satirist, Sydney Smith, led the attack on such attitudes in the radical *Edinburgh Review*. He had written ten thousand Latin verses at school "and no man in his sense would dream in after life of ever making another. So much for life and time wasted." Such work made school "irksome and detested slavery". Later, Benthamite critics suggested that "the memory, the attention and the taste may be cultivated by useful as well as by useless knowledge."

The discipline of the schools was also attacked. Pastoral care by masters was harsh yet casual. Headmasters were still great floggers. The notorious Dr. Keate of Eton was the greatest. "He was little more than five feet in height," wrote A. W. Kingslake, his former pupil, "but within this space was concentrated the pluck of ten battalions." After a cheating incident he beat seventy-two boys. "It was a grand scene in the library", wrote Kingslake. "The floor was covered with victims; the benches and tables with spectators ... jeers and laughter accompanied the execution." Such brutality was the result of high pupil-teacher ratios. Keate, for example, tried to teach two hundred boys at once. Lessons were interrupted by "a kind of humming noise with the lips closed, so that the culprits could not be discovered", or by boys who sang and threw books. Yet the masters wanted no change: the more pupils they had in their classes, the greater their fees.

By 1800 an unwritten system of "boy rule" had evolved. It was not considered right for masters to interfere in their pupils' lives.

They should not, said a Headmaster, "be spies, coercing freedom of speech and action." The influence of his peers became a major element in the boy's school life. He was "roughed into manhood" in a school world that was a miniature of society itself. As he fought for status among his fellows, he evolved "superior manliness, generosity and self-control". His rise to leadership at school anticipated his later progress in life. "Alexander at the head of the world", commented the writer Horace Walpole in a letter, "never tasted the true pleasure that boys have enjoyed at the head of a school. Little intrigues, little schemes and policies engage their thoughts ... they are laying the foundation for their middle age of life."

Clearer eyes saw the uglier side of "boy rule". Bullying was rife. Small boys were tossed in blankets in the dormitories, one being scalped by a bedpost as he fell. Others were forced to toast bread with their bare hands. A Christ's Hospital boy was branded. A Westminster pupil, J. Froude, remembered, "We were flung in together to fight our own way ... When I had crawled to bed ... I have been woken many times by the hot points of cigars burning holes in my face." Eton produced a "regular and permanent system of unrelenting persecution". Long Chamber, where boys slept, locked in without supervision, was notorious. The Etonian, Edward Thring, recalled his memories of: "the great bare dirty room ... Who can ever forget that know it, the wild, rough, rollicking freedom, the frolic and fun of that land of misrule, with its strange code of traditional boy law?"

Fagging was a variant of bullying. "Fags" were called after the "bearers of faggots" who had served the fires in medieval schools, to spare the cost of proper servants. Younger boys served the older ones, cleaning and running errands. Radical opinion saw fagging as a symbol of upper-class tyranny. "To black shoes under penalty of being beaten for non-compliance, is slavery in man or boy", claimed a *Westminster Review* writer. Fags were "passive, obedient menials of a set of premature despots". Public schools were "models of instruction in arbitrary power and abject slavery".

Critics also deplored the lack of supervision of spare time in the schools. Eton boys could gamble on cock-fighting, go racing, drink in taverns. Confined in the City, Westminster boys were notorious for their violence, as they terrorized local people. In country districts, boys went poaching, even hunted with their own dog packs. Frequent roll-calls, or extra lessons in "accomplishments" did not prevent idleness. The novelist, Henry Fielding, had called the public schools "the nurseries of all vice and immorality". By 1800 many critics agreed with him.

Conservatism of pupils hindered change. The turn of the century saw revolts in all the great schools. Although boys were influenced by the French Revolution, sometimes affecting the red cap of liberty, they really fought to maintain the old order in school life. Winchester had its "Great Rebellion" in 1793, when some boys had pistols and hurled stones from a tower; and another in 1818, when pupils, objecting to the Headmaster's "spying", were only quelled by soldiers with bayonets. At Harrow, in 1808, senior boys paraded banners inscribed "Liberty and Rebellion", as a protest against curtailment of their flogging powers. Rugby had a revolt in 1797, when boys blew up the Headmaster's door, and had to be calmed by the Riot Act.

Old Boys, too, prevented reform. The vogue for sentimental nostalgia for school days was already strong. "What Etonian was ever lukewarm in the panegyric of the scene of his boyish delights?" wrote a correspondent to *New Monthly* magazine in 1824. "To the latest period of existence ... his eye will beam with renovated lustre in reverting to the day when he 'urged the flying ball' and 'cleft the glassy wave' in those favourite haunts." Such sentimentalists saw school tradition as "sacred and hallowed", and therefore unalterable.

Bold Headmasters had already tried reform. Thomas James, Head of Rugby from 1778 to 1794, was a skilled organizer, who had devised tutorial systems, experimented with non-classical subjects, and given the boys individual study rooms to improve accommodation. His former pupil Samuel Butler revived Shrewsbury (which he found "shrunk to scarcely a single boy") after 1798: his school became distinguished for examination successes, and for the revival of the old "praeposter" or prefect system, used long ago at Winchester, which gave older boys a share in school authority.

Such reforms were local attempts to modify schools. What was needed was a fresh purpose and spirit throughout the system. In the dawning Victorian age—sober and self-righteous—criticism of decadent schools sharpened. "Before an Eton Boy is ready for University," suggested a writer in *The Quarterly Journal of*

Education in 1834, "he may have acquired at a place of education ... a confirmed taste for gluttony and drunkenness, an aptitude for brutal sports and a passion for female society of the most degrading kind ..." Something better was obviously needed. The reforming influence of Thomas Arnold (1795–1842) provided it.

He was Headmaster of Rugby from 1828 to 1842. On his appointment, it was the aimless brutality of school life that concerned him. His stated intention was to create "a place of Christian Education, to form Christian men". His list of priorities was therefore strikingly novel: "First, religious and moral principle; second, gentlemanly conduct; thirdly, intellectual ability."

The chapel sermon was the heart of his work. His pupil, Thomas Hughes, recalled Arnold's talks to the school: "The tall, gallant form, the kindling eye, the voice, now soft as the low notes of a flute, now clear and stirring as the call of a light infantry bugle." His themes were "common faults which you every day commit, common feelings which every day pass through your hearts and minds," which he related to Christianity. His personality was enough to influence most boys and to dominate the more sensitive of his Sixth Formers. Pupils never forgot his "ashy paleness" when he was angry, or "the black cloud" that came into his face when discussing authors or historical figures he disliked.

Arnold's ideal assistant was "an active man ... a Christian and a Gentleman". Staff meetings and proper salaries advanced the status of his chosen men. Boarding houses were removed from the traditional care of "dames" and passed to masters, giving each "a horse of his own to ride". Yet Arnold's real agents were his Sixth Form boys, the "praeposters" to whom he gave authority, asking service in return. He shrewdly realized that boys were more impressed by older school fellows than by masters. A good example from the Sixth Form would raise the tone of the whole school. The senior boys were to be "like officers in the army whose want of moral courage would be thought cowardice".

Arnold was not widely admired in his own day. There were arguments with the town about the exclusion of local boys; a case of unjust flogging was reported in the paper; his many public writings on church and state affairs were regarded with suspicion as "the language of heresy". He himself was disappointed with his work, and, at the time of his sudden death in 1842, he could not have guessed at his future fame.

Appreciation of his work spread gradually. Oxford tutors became aware of unusual undergraduates, "thoughtful, manly-minded, conscious of duty and obligation." These were the "bearded sages", Rugby boys indoctrinated by Arnold. They in turn became masters, taking their Arnoldian ideas into other schools. Reform spread. A French visitor to Eton in the 1860s noted that almost all boys were religious and said their prayers.

The writings of disciples created the Arnold legend. A favourite pupil, Arthur Stanley, published his *Life of Thomas Arnold* in 1844, making his master a giant of the educational world. Matthew Arnold's poem, "Rugby Chapel" (1857) described his father as a "soul tempered with fire", an inspiration to the age. It was, however, a popular novel that made Arnold known to a huge public. *Tom Brown's Schooldays* by Thomas Hughes was published in 1857. It was an immediate success, hailed as "a capital book ... a spirited record of genuine schoolboy life". *The Times* thought it "the truest, liveliest and most sympathising description of a unique phase of English life that has yet been given to the public." Hughes described Tom's progress from his astonishing first day at Rugby to becoming "the brave, helpful truth-telling Englishman and a Christian", that Arnold's influence made him. If Hughes distorted Arnold's ideals, he also translated them into practical terms that persuaded generations of parents that public school was just the training they wanted for their sons.

Coincident with Arnold's work were other social factors that saved the public schools from collapse or suggested government control, and stimulated a rapid growth of the system from 1840 to 1860. There was a wider clientele. Newly-rich parents, who had made fortunes in the Industrial Revolution, wanted their sons to rise socially. On the other hand, they wanted value for money. Some of the older schools seemed too crowded and expensive. There was room, therefore, for new and cheaper boarding schools, to which the ever-growing railway system could carry sons of ambitious parents.

There were various kinds of foundation. The proprietary school was already a popular device. The school was set up as a company with wealthy local people investing in it by buying shares, so receiving the right to nominate pupils. Cheltenham College (1841) was a successful example of this "joint stock education". Its founders, retired civil servants and military men, were unashamedly biased in favour of wealthy parents. "Had we admitted tradesmen in any instance", wrote the College Secretary, "we should have had the sons of gentlemen shaking hands perhaps with schoolfellows behind the counter." The curriculum was "fitted for life", preparing boys for Church, Army, the Law; even Sanskrit and Hindustani were taught to candidates for the Indian Civil Service. Helped by the railway boom, the college grew rapidly. Its discipline, however, was in the old style: one runaway was so severely caned that his jacket was cut to pieces. Other proprietary schools, such as Marlborough (1843), intended for clergymen's sons, or Epsom (1853) for doctors' sons, were set up for particular parental professional groups.

The Oxford Movement had its influence on school foundation. Various denominations set up their own schools. Thus the Leys School in Cambridge and Taunton School had non-conformist origins; Ratcliffe and Beaumont were Catholic schools.

The most remarkable agent of such church activity was a clergyman, Nathaniel Woodard (1811–91). He saw ignorance as a threat to Christian civilization. In a pamphlet, *A Plea for the Middle Classes* (1848) he set out an ambitious plan for a network of boarding schools to meet the needs of three carefully-defined levels of the neglected middle-class. Such schools would be "cells" from which the nation's spiritual life would be regenerated.

Woodard gradually built a small empire of seventeen schools, thanks to his extraordinary talent for fund raising. Near his Sussex home he founded a three-tier system: Lancing College (1848) for the rich or professional parent; Hurstpierpoint (1849) for "superior tradesmen" and farmers; Ardingly (1858) for "small tradesmen". Ardingly was to be what Gladstone called "Mr. Woodard's *Great Eastern*", with room for a thousand pupils.

A unique foundation was Wellington (1859). The Queen and leading Ministers had believed that a school for "orphan children of indigent and meritorious officers of the Army" would be a suitable memorial to the hero of Waterloo. The first Headmaster was able to change the "charity school" for "scrubby little orphans"—a concept disliked by the Wellington Family—by admitting rich boys as fee-payers. Wellington found a strong link with nearby Sandhurst in preparing boys for Army careers.

In such various ways, thirty-one public schools were started between 1840 and 1869.Their Headmasters worked to place their schools among the Great Schools of England.

Grammar schools and private academies

Educational opportunities for middle-class families existed outside the public schools.

Many grammar schools survived, their fortunes varying according to their position or the value of the original endowment. A dynamic Headmaster could win his school a high reputation. In the 1780s William Taylor stressed mathematics and Newtonian physics at Hawkshead Grammar school in Cumberland, attended by the poet, William Wordsworth. The school drew boys from all over north-west England. Other schools, described in contemporary surveys, simply wasted away. In 1780, Shaftesbury School closed for lack of pupils; Sherborne had "not one boarder left but very few day scholars". Several schools were "not kept up for many years past", becoming "empty walls without scholars". Dishonest masters, with comfortable sinecures, pocketed the endowment money. The master at Monk's Kirby, Warwickshire, was "most illiterate and unfit for the office. He attends occasionally at the school 'where he has nothing to do'."

The classical curriculum was the main cause of this decay. Although more utilitarian subjects were increasingly valued, it needed a decree of Chancery or private Act of Parliament to widen the range of a grammar school's teaching. Thus at Macclesfield in Cheshire, an Act allowed teaching "not only in grammar and classical learning, but also in writing, arithmetic, navigation, mathematics (and) the modern languages." Sometimes "English" schools to teach modern subjects were set up beside the original building. Such reforms were hindered by a famous legal judgement of 1805. The Governors of Leeds Grammar School wished to use part of the endowment for modern studies; the Headmaster refused to change. When the issue was contested in court, Lord Chancellor Eldon declared that a grammar school was "for teaching grammatically the learned languages according to Dr. Johnson's definition". Teaching anything at Leeds but "the learned tongues" was illegal. Eldon's judgement crippled the grammar schools until an Act of 1840 allowed them a wider curriculum. Attempts to divert endowments to new purposes also failed. Henry Brougham's effort of 1820 to use such endowment funds to set up schools for the poor was coldly received. The Headmaster of Tonbridge declared that grammar schools were for boys "with talents and diligence, who can live without manual labour". For the poor boy, "the humble schools prepared for him are sufficient."

A picture of grammar school life in 1800 was left by a Manchester pupil, Samuel Bamford. In the single schoolroom, by a "red cheerful fire", sat the master with "a newspaper or two ... a couple of canes with the ends split, and a medley of boys' playthings, such as tops, whips, marbles, apple scrapers, nutcrackers ..." There were six classes, studying Latin, the Bible and spelling. Each sat on its "strong oaken bench", with backs against panelled walls. Boys were placed by proficiency, not by age. Order was maintained by force; pupils at Leeds were beaten with "a piece of slate frame".

New foundations deliberately opposed the decayed grammar school tradition. An important innovator was the non-conformist Mill Hill (1807), heir to the Dissenting Academies, with its influential building and its "modern curriculum". The utilitarian mood of the 1820s produced remarkable proprietary schools that promised cheap, efficient education coloured by ideas from Prussian High Schools. The Liverpool Institute (1825) led the way, but University College School (1828) and other London schools proved more important, as practical reaction against the "barbarous" public schools. Their "Grecian" style of architecture reflected the contemporary "blaze of light and knowledge" as opposed to the "dark monastic exploded institutions of our country". Individual classrooms allowed class teaching as opposed to the self-tuition of the public school, where according to the Head of Leicester Proprietary School "more than half the time of a pupil is spent in groping out for himself the substance of his lesson."

There were also thousands of private schools described by a contemporary as "the common medium of instruction for the children of our middle classes". The vogue had begun after 1750. An eighteenth century teacher, John Clarke, had written of the "promiscuous, numerous herd of rude, wild boys, many of them very vicious" at large public schools, and had praised the twenty-pupil private academy. A German visitor, Pastor Moritz, noted "a prodigious number" of such little schools in the 1780s. In the better ones he found "a kind of family education, which is certainly the most natural if properly conducted". Early nineteenth century newspapers were crowded with their advertisements, full of extravagant promises. There were classical schools, conducted by Anglican clergymen, like that described in George Eliot's *Mill on the Floss* (1860) where Tom Tulliver learned only Latin, finding "an

34

elaborate appliance of unintelligible ideas and ... much failure in the effort to learn by rote". Then there were Academies, which prided themselves on their "practical studies"—mathematics, science and English instead of "polite literature". Too often this kind of "useful knowledge" replaced one pedantry by another. A hundred-page popular manual *An Easy Introduction to the Arts and Sciences* (1821) dealt in question-and-answer style with an ambitious range of topics: religion, morality, painting, architecture, law, medicine, geography and so on. Such "reformed" teaching material could hardly challenge the "useless" classics. Nevertheless grammar school men looked jealously at the best of these academies, which the Head of Tonbridge dismissed as "commercial schools for the shop, the warehouse, the counting house and the manufactory".

The worst private schools were well described in nineteenth century novels. Charles Dickens wrote bitterly of his London school, Wellington House Academy, in *David Copperfield* (1850) and the essay "Our School". There was the owner "always ruling ciphering books with a bloated mahogany ruler, or smiting the palms of offenders with the same diabolical instrument." There was the Latin Master, "a doubled-up near-sighted man with a crutch ... always putting onions into his ears for deafness." There was the "forlorn and desolate schoolroom, bristling with pegs for hats and slates ... Scraps of old copy-books and exercises litter the dirty floor ... There is a strange unwholesome smell upon the room, like mildewed corduroys ... sweet apples, wanting air, and rotten books."

Blackest of all were the notorious Yorkshire schools, exposed by Dickens in *Nicholas Nickleby* (1839). Newspaper notices for these schools, with the sinister promise, "no vacations", attracted his notice. He found that unwanted children could be sent to be boarded permanently with those "ignorant, coarse, brutal men", the Yorkshire schoolmasters. In 1838, Dickens went to examine schools near Barnard Castle. His own monstrous Mr. Squeers was based on a certain Shaw of Bowes Academy. *Nicholas Nickleby* led to the closure of such cruel parodies of schools.

The best private schools carried out remarkable experiments in organization and teaching method. At William Gilpin's Cheam School in Surrey, which flourished in the 1780s, plots of the school garden could be legally conveyed from boy to boy, or grouped as estates to be let to tenants, giving experience of land management.

There was a code of laws with trials by boy juries. At David Williams's Chelsea Academy (1773) teaching experiment concerned with the "management of curiosity", used projects integrating various subjects based on a "concentric system", examining the garden, then the neighbourhood, district, country, continent. Older pupils became sufficiently knowledgeable to read over papers of the Royal Society. Williams sat in classes given by assistants to test his theories. His writings won him a European reputation.

Hazelwood school in Birmingham, run by the celebrated Hill family from 1819 to 1833, was unique. After experiments at Hill Top school, Thomas Wright Hill and his five sons (among them Rowland, founder of the Penny Post, and Matthew, reformer of English criminal law) moved to the purpose-built Hazelwood, which included such novelties as a stage, museum, swimming pool and astronomical observatory.

A wide curriculum aimed to produce "men of business". Attention was given to motivation of all pupils and academic studies were balanced by "voluntary labour" (practical hobbies such as printing, mapping, model-making, work on school magazines, and reporting on debates or school trials). What the Hills called "the noble art of money making" lay behind rewards for work. Marks consisted of token coinage issued by a boy banker. There were the "prime" (1 mark), "decad" (10) and "cent" (100). All could aspire to win the brass "quingent" (500) or copper "chiliad" (1000) or even a real silver medal. Money could buy food or free time; bankrupts worked off debts in detention.

Complex rules governed the boys' days. Punctuality, "the regular and systematic disposal of time", was valued. A bugler began the day at 6 a.m.; thereafter boys moved on the sound of a bell to the music of a band. Movement to lessons was timed (to the second) by strokes on a drum. A monitor, the "silentiary", who wore slippers and special hat, controlled noise. Offenders against school laws were tried by elected pupil judges: penalties were fines or confinement in a dark cupboard, the Hills disapproving of corporal punishment.

The Hills' book, *Public Education* (1825) attracted wide interest and influenced Thomas Arnold. The fine detail of their system made it inimitable. Hazelwood was rather soulless, forcing boys into premature manhood. There were hints of healthy boys' reactions: marks were stolen or even counterfeited. Yet the school was justly described by the writer Thomas de Quincey as "the most original experiment in education which in this country at least has been attempted."

Beyond these practical experiments were the projects of dreamers such as Robert Pemberton, a follower of Robert Owen. His book *The Happy Colony* (1854) proposed a classless society in New Zealand. At the centre of the capital city (built in concentric circles) would be "the Elysian Academy", educating all young people up to twenty-one. Vast museums would provide specimens of every branch of learning and craft. Pupils would learn eight languages, ready to communicate with the entire world. Plans got no further than giant paintings, displayed at a meeting in 1855, which discussed what *The Times* called "a host of visionary and impractical schemes".

Schooling for girls

For centuries, marriage and domestic life had been considered the only roles suitable for women of upper and middle classes. Any education they received had been to fit them for these roles.

Briefly, the bright intellectual world of Tudor times had managed to admire the female scholar. Mary and Elizabeth, daughters of Henry VIII, had been accomplished linguists; to Lady Jane Grey, "Sport in the park is but a shadow of that pleasure that I find in Plato." The royal tutor thought that "women should study wisdom, which doth instruct their manners and inform their living."

In the seventeenth and eighteenth centuries, female learning went out of fashion. "She-clerks" and "blue-stockings" were regarded as ludicrous. "Accomplishments"—lady-like skills that would "increase a young lady's chance of a prize in the matrimonial lottery"—became the centre of female education. Boarding schools became a vogue from the Restoration period onwards. Here girls learned some reading, writing and scripture, but concentrated on music, dancing, domestic skills, and "curious works of the needle". The "phrenzy of accomplishments" dotted the country with these boarding schools. Eighteenth century Brighton boasted many such little "Academies". In 1759, a *London Chronicle* writer noted how, in villages near London, "There are one or two little boarding schools with an inscription over the door, 'Young ladies boarded and educated' ... Hither the blacksmith, the ale-house keeper, the shoemaker etc. sends his daughter, who, from the moment she enters these walls, becomes a young lady."

There was great variety among these schools. At the Queen's Square school in London, the "Young Ladies' Eton", fifteen-year-old girls wore full eighteenth century fashion with hair powder and rouge. They practised the arts of greeting acquaintances, of paying visits, of writing elegant letters. A coach was kept nearby so that girls could learn to get in and out, "with calmness and grace, and without any unnecessary display of ankles". At another extreme was the little school, the small business venture, where a dozen girls were boarded. Fiction provides pictures of these: Mrs. Goddard, in Jane Austen's *Emma* (1816), kept "a real, honest, old-fashioned boarding school, where a reasonable quantity of accomplishments were sold at a reasonable price, and where girls might be sent out of the way and scramble themselves into a little education without any danger of coming back prodigies."

There were also wretched schools, attacked by a clergyman, J. Chirol, in 1809. The poor health bred in such establishments earned them "the dreadful denomination of 'the ante-chambers of death' ". The grim picture of Lowood school in Charlotte Bronte's *Jane Eyre* (1847) was based on her own experience at Cowan Bridge, in Yorkshire. The childhood deaths of her elder sisters, Maria and Elizabeth, were hastened by conditions at the school.

Girls were taught through dreary catechisms of knowledge like the best-selling *Historical and Miscellaneous Questions for the use of Young People* (1800) by Miss Richmal Magnal.

"Q. What is whale bone?

A. A sort of gristle found inside the whale in long, flat pieces.

Q. What is whalebone used for?

A. To stiffen stays, umbrellas and whips."

There was "use of the globes" and such futile activities as learning pages of *Johnson's Dictionary* by heart.

In a school world where "an advantageous settlement in marriage is the prize", great attention was given to deportment and posture. Girls were laced into constricting stays, some even sleeping in them to "acquire the fascinating undulations that Art affords to Nature". Backboards were common to pull back the shoulders. Short girls suffered the agonies of "swinging by the head", intended to stretch the body.

Punishment aimed to humiliate the pupil. At a Brighton school there was a Saturday "Judgement Day". A pupil, Frances Cobbe, remembered "nine young ladies obliged to sit for hours in the angles of three rooms, with their faces to the wall, half of them being quite of marriageable age." At an Isle of Wight school the penalty for a lie was to wear a black gown with a red tongue, marked "LIAR", sewn on the front.

Many middle-class girls were educated at home. This could be stimulating in a large family with thoughtful parents, with much reading aloud and discussion. Sometimes girls shared lessons with their brothers' tutor, or had a governess. Such a post was the only paid employment for a girl from poor but genteel background. Pay was poor: an advertisement in *The Times* of 1843 offered only £12 a year to a governess "of lady-like manners, capable of imparting a sound English education with French, music, and singing, dancing and drawing." Her status was that of a higher servant, with life divided between school-room and garret. The governess had few intellectual pretensions, having been inadequately taught herself. Most were sad victims of the surplus of women. Their fate was grim. Florence Nightingale saw them dying in her "Institution for the Care of Sick Gentlewomen". "The deep feeling I have of the miserable position of educated women in England was gained while I was there", she wrote in a letter.

Advocates of a more meaningful education for girls were regarded as cranks. Maria Edgeworth, in *Practical Education* (1798), asserted that "it will tend to the happiness of society in general that women should have their understanding cultivated." Mary Wollstonecraft's *Vindication of the Rights of Women* (1792) was a fiercer demand that women should be considered men's equals. Co-educational schools should be the basis of a revolution in attitude. By the 1830s, such opinions seemed less eccentric. The *Quarterly Journal of Education* of 1831 advocated girls' schools, under government control, graded according to social class. Women writers protested against the elevation of "the ornamental above useful acquirements" in girls' studies. Yet a widely-read authoress, Mrs. William Ellis, was able to tell girls, in her *Daughters of England* (1843), that they should be "content to be inferior to men— inferior in mental power in the same proportion that you are inferior in bodily strength." Such was the conservative climate in which the Victorian reformers of girls' education began their work.

A young Englishman goes to school at six or seven years old; and he remains in a course of education till twenty-three ... in all that time his sole and exclusive occupation is learning Latin and Greek; he has scarcely a notion that there is any other kind of excellence; and the great system of facts with which he is the most perfectly acquainted are the intrigues of the heathen Gods: with whom Pan slept?—with whom Jupiter?—whom Apollo ravished?

SYDNEY SMITH
The Edinburgh Review (1810)

There are at this present writing five hundred boys at Eton, kicked and licked, and bullied by another hundred—scrubbing shoes, running errands, making false concords and ... putting their posteriors on a block for Dr. Hawtrey to lash at; and still calling it education. They are proud of it—Good heavens!—absolutely vain of it ... They call it the good old English system.

WILLIAM MAKEPEACE THACKERAY
Irish Sketch Book (1842)

My dear dear mother,
If you don't let me come home, I die—I am all over ink, and my fine clothes have been spoilt. I have been tost in a blanket, and seen a ghost.

I remain, my dear, dear mother,
Your dutiful and most unhappy son,
Freddy.

Letter from a Westminster schoolboy (early nineteenth century)

If Arnold were elected, he would change the face of education all through the public schools of England.

THE PROVOST OF ORIEL COLLEGE, OXFORD
Testimonial for Thomas Arnold's application to Rugby (1828)

A most singular and striking change has come upon our public schools ... I am sure that to Dr. Arnold's personal earnest simplicity, strength of character, power of influence and piety ... the carrying of this improvement into our schools is mainly attributable. He was the first ...

DR. MOBERLEY
Headmaster of Winchester (1842)

Whoever will examine the state of the grammar schools in different parts of this kingdom will see to what a lamentable condition most of them are reduced ... empty walls without scholars, and everything neglected but the receipt of the salaries and emoluments.

LORD CHIEF JUSTICE KENYON
Comment on a dispute at Skipton Grammar School (1795)

It glows with hot runs at hare and hounds. It is "swinky" with glorious innings, leg-hits for six, drives for four, sweet chisels to cover-point ... It shakes with cheers for two school-house matches at football, won running ... It is cool with pleasant baths under the alders in the steaming summer. It luxuriates in that righteous licking of the bully, Flashman ... it has a jolly smell of frying sausages, and altogether is the sort of book that elderly maiden ladies might not like.

DUBLIN UNIVERSITY MAGAZINE
Review of *Tom Brown's Schooldays* (1857)

By juries and committees, by marks and by appeals to a sense of honour, discipline was maintained. But this was done, I think, at too great a sacrifice: the thoughtlessness, the spring, the elation of childhood were taken from us; we were premature men ... The school forced us into a precocious imitation of maturity.

WILLIAM SARGENT, a Hazelwood boy
Essays of a Birmingham Manufacturer (1869)

My two girls have had pretty good education ... they can read, write and cast accompts; they understand their needles, broadstitch, cross and change, and all manner of plain work; they can pink, point and frill; and know something of music; they can do up small cloaths, work upon cat-gut. My eldest can cut paper, and my youngest has a very pretty manner of telling fortunes upon the cards.

OLIVER GOLDSMITH
The Vicar of Wakefield (1766)

Oh mothers, will you ... continue to be the wilful instruments of the ruin of your daughters—Nay—I tremble while I write it—nay—their murderers, by sending them to those hotbeds of vice and self-destruction,—the boarding schools?

J. CHIROL
An Enquiry into the Best System of Female Education (1809)

Why the disposition of knowledge between the two sexes should be so great, when the inequality in natural talents is so small, and why the understanding of women should be lavished on trifles, when nature has made it capable of higher and better things, we profess ourselves not able to understand.

SYDNEY SMITH
Essays (1818)

3 Elementary education for all: 1870–1902

The 1870 Education Act

The late 1860s produced a climate favourable for wider state intervention in elementary schooling. "Throughout the length and breadth of our nation a sense of weariness with old organisations ... works and grows", wrote Matthew Arnold in *Culture and Anarchy* (1869). Younger teams of politicians, led by Gladstone and Disraeli, emerged to lead in re-consideration of social and political problems.

Public debate produced fresh arguments to support educational reform. Rapid population growth (11.9 per cent increase between 1851 and 1861, for example) made the industrial towns teem with poor children, vividly described by Dickens and Mayhew. Inspectors realized that few attended school, spending the day "idling about the streets, learning nothing but evil and acquiring habits which utterly unfit them for honest labour." Church societies had not the resources to build schools where they were most needed, in the industrial slums. Even Edward Baines, leader of the Voluntaryists, was forced to concede in 1867 that state intervention was now necessary.

There were economic arguments. England, so recently "Workshop of the World", seemed to be losing ground in international industrial competition. At the Paris International Fair of 1867, English products won only ten of ninety sections. English exhibits were described as "slovenly intruded heaps of raw material mingled with pieces of rusty iron". The sophisticated, educated worker was becoming more valuable to employers. As farming became mechanized, the employer found ignorant workers a handicap. A *Times* correspondent wrote, concerning a farming exhibition: "Of the mass of machines exhibited ... how many ...

have in their labourers the skill and patience to work and keep them in order?"

The shadow of war was another stimulus to reform. The educated soldier, it seemed, won battles. The victorious Northern troops in the United States, and the all-conquering Prussian soldiers, came from societies where schooling was an accepted necessity. The much-discussed Prussian victories in France during 1870 were a potent influence on public opinion. "It is ignorance that has lost France", declared a French politician.

Religious bigotry was in decline. The public was becoming less patient with the "religious difficulty", which killed several Bills in the 1860s. The *Edinburgh Review* spoke of "the intolerable cant of the religionists". Practical parents already chose "a good plain useful education with little care about religious distinctions".

There were political factors too. Disraeli's Reform Act of 1867, his famous "leap in the dark", which had given the vote to virtually all male householders, doubled the franchise overnight. Robert Lowe, in 1868, warned that these new voters were "growing up in vice and ignorance", and that Parliament should now "educate our masters".

The widened electorate of 1868 returned a Liberal Government "ardent for reform". A speaker in Parliament noted that "the present time is favourable for the passing of a wise, a large and well considered measure for the education of the people."

Gladstone appointed W. E. Forster (1819–86) to supervise this initiative. He had been a successful wool merchant, who had started schools at his mill and in the Leeds slums, having long been convinced of "the right of the English workman to demand an education for his children". His marriage to Thomas Arnold's daughter brought him the expert private advice of her brother, Matthew Arnold.

As Forster prepared his Bill, opinion in the country polarized around large pressure groups. The Birmingham Education League (1869) demanded free, compulsory, state schooling for all, free from religious colouring. It was supported by extremist non-conformists, Liberals and Trades Unionists. The National Education Union, formed in opposition, supported by Church of England and Conservative interests, fought to protect church schools. Forster's task was to forge a compromise from these extremes.

Inspectors were sent to report on schooling in Birmingham,

Leeds, Liverpool and Manchester. Only a third of four million working-class children attended any school. Many were in the streets, learning only "vagrancy, mendicancy and crime". Private schools "conducted in cellars and other filthy places", were conducted by teachers "physically, morally or intellectually disqualified for any office", whose teaching was "deplorably bad." Distribution of church schools was haphazard. Only Roman Catholics supplied funds adequate to support their schools. The Report concluded that voluntary effort was not enough; that to bring "efficient elementary education within the reach of every home, some further and powerful impulse must be given to its working ..."

Forster introduced his Bill in February 1870. England's survival as an industrial power and parliamentary democracy depended on the provision of education for the whole population. He therefore had two aims: "To cover the country with good schools" and "To get the parents to send their children to these schools".

He proposed a compromise plan, devised with considerable political skill. The country was to be divided into school districts, based on civil parishes and the boroughs. London was to be one mighty unit. Each district was to be surveyed to see if its "educational condition" was adequate. Where schooling was "sufficient, efficient and suitable", no action would be taken; where it was not, a School Board would be set up to create and run state elementary schools, financed by a local rate, government grant and "school pence" from pupils.

The churches were placated in various ways. Voluntary agencies were given six months to build church schools in ill-provided areas before any School Board was established. There was to be "Christian training" in the Board schools, based on "simple Bible teaching". Such lessons were placed at the beginning and end of the day, when parents with conscientious objections might easily withdraw their children. A crucial clause, added by William Cowper-Temple declared that "no religious catechism or religious formulary, which is distinctive of any particular denomination, shall be taught in the school." Thus the chief stumbling block for previous Bills was surmounted.

Forster's Act became law on August 9, 1870. It created the "dual system" of Board and Church elementary schools, which brought some schooling within reach of every English child. There was some bitterness at this "compromise upon a compromise" among supporters of the League that caused a serious split in the Liberal party. Churchmen, by contrast, spoke against the "godless" Board schools. However, the 1870 Act was to prove one of the most significant pieces of Victorian social reform, as the seed from which the mighty oak of state education grew. Forster seemed to be aware of the potential of his work. When he left office in 1874, he wrote: "Some education is now secured to all English children. Whether that some is enough to be of real value is now the question, but I do not think the work can stop."

Elementary education in the School Board era

The last thirty years of the nineteenth century saw the rapid spread of efficient elementary schooling. There were one million pupils in inspected schools in 1870: six million by 1900. After a frenzy of church activity in the six months after the 1870 Act (in which 3,342 applications for building grants were made), voluntary effort gradually faded, dependent as it was upon the uncertainties of private subscription. The Board schools came to challenge Church supremacy in numbers, claiming nearly half the elementary population by 1900, and to surpass it in quality of teachers, buildings and equipment.

The School Boards were a striking innovation in English life. They were necessary at a time when local government was either lacking or distrusted. Each Board, containing from five to fifteen members, was to be elected by local ratepayers to hold office for three years. Working-class and women candidates were eligible. The Board had the power to raise rates, buy land and borrow money to build its schools.

The Boards aroused much interest, bringing "primary democracy" to districts that had never known any democratic organization. Seats on Boards became highly coveted, attracting candidates "of high class ... men and women of strong philanthropic instincts". Their work let them see the reality of working-class life and "the misery of ignorance". "The persons who will henceforth undergo the strictest process of education are members of the School Boards themselves", noted the *School Board Chronicle* in 1871.

Non-conformist areas were quickest to act. Cornwall was first to open a Board school, and had ninety Boards by 1878. By contrast, Conservative Berkshire had only seven. Certain areas fought off Boards: the Bishop of Ely gathered funds to save Cambridgeshire for the Church. Chester, York, Winchester and Windsor also resisted. The 2,500 Boards varied in size and power. There was the mighty London Board, serving four million people, of which it was written (in *The Times*): "No equally powerful body will exist in England outside Parliament." By contrast, Thorngumbauld in Yorkshire served only 536 people. Whereas the London Board met at Guildhall, with a clerk costing £800 a year to take its minutes, Bangor Board bought a minute book, a "strong tin box" and a seal, and was ready for work. The Boards were united by their paper, *The School Board Chronicle* and by correspondence.

Their first task was to survey local needs. This entailed counting children, a complicated task in large cities. In London, Inspectors sought out the homeless "street Arabs", who lived "in railway arches ... in the cellars of unfinished houses, or wherever the homeless offspring of destitute poverty may stealthily creep." It was found that London alone contained half a million children not at school. Until buildings were ready, temporary schools were set up in huts and halls. In *Schools and Scholars* (1886) James Runciman described the stress of work as a pioneer London Board teacher. In a "long hideous drill room", he began to teach "dirty, foul-mouthed blackguards, little Yahoos", who came "not from homes, but from lairs". They were swarming with vermin, or deformed by hunger. They were unable to concentrate or accept any discipline: "A boy thought nothing of rising from a desk and wriggling along the floor to pick up a marble or any stray object that took his interest." Singing seemed the only way to quieten the pupils. After school, Runciman was exhausted: "He loathed the sight of food and only a long resolute walk in the open enabled him to shake off the weariness of nerve." The missionary zeal of pioneer teachers was thus tempered by classes of a hundred or more children. An idea of their behaviour is given by a list of habits to cure, drawn up by an H.M.I.: "Spitting on the floor without putting the foot on it, picking the nose, cleaning the boots on the dress, wiping the pen ... by sucking it, drawing it through the hair, rubbing it on the dress."

Resentment against the Board schools was strong in some areas. Parents were used to child labour. H. Philpott, in *London at School* (1904), recalled "seeing the corridor thronged with men and women who had come to demand their children at the stroke of twelve or four-thirty ... They would argue, 'He's been putting money into your pocket; now I want him to put some into mine ...'" Teachers were attacked: a knowledge of boxing was considered necessary to a man in rough districts. Parents complained about school discipline: "I should like to know how much more spite you intend to put upon my child", wrote one. "I think you had better hang her and be done with it." Gradually the schools won favour. Parents took pride in their children's learning; teachers helped poor families by collecting money, making clothes, writing letters for them after school hours. Most trying for teachers were clashes with local clergymen, who illogically regarded the Board schools as their preserve, and who complained of their "atheism".

The large Boards eventually produced outstanding buildings. The first purpose-built London Board school opened in Whitechapel in 1873, important guests struggling through the washing that festooned local lanes. Such early schools were mere three-deck blocks of rooms, sometimes with a roof playground, squeezed onto small, expensive sites. Later, the London Board architect, E. R. Robson, introduced novelties into England from the impressive High Schools of Prussia: the central hall, with surrounding classrooms opening off corridors. The distinctive façades were based on "the old brick architecture of London", in Queen Anne style, in reaction to the Gothic of Church schools. "The building then approaches more nearly the spirit of our own time," wrote Robson, in *School Architecture* (1874). "Whether we like it or not, the education of the people is now governed by the lawyer rather than the clergyman." These tall, solid buildings dominated the townscape, "rising above the slates, like brick islands in a lead-coloured sea", (as Sir Arthur Conan Doyle described them). Other cities followed London's lead. Outside the towns, large schools were rare. Most children still studied in the single school-room, shivering in winter if placed far from the central stove, stifled in summer by poor ventilation, sometimes crammed in the old galleries of the 1820s.

The School Boards improved the status of the teacher. Salary scales and formal procedures replaced the capricious rule of clerical managers. The National Union of Elementary Teachers (later the N.U.T.) was formed in 1870 to allow teachers "to give expression to their opinions" and "take united action in any matter affecting their interests". Their magazine, *The Schoolmaster,* claimed in 1872 that "teachers generally should awake to a sense of their power. Few classes of the community could exert more influence in a contested election than teachers."

The huge rise in pupil numbers forced expedients on the authorities to increase the teaching force: examination pass standards were lowered, or certificates granted after one year's training. The Church societies opened more colleges. Life for the trainee remained bleak. James Runciman remembered Borough Road in London with its "barren foetid rooms, with their greasy forms and notched desks". He hated the lack of privacy, especially on Sundays when "the sickly rooms depressed the very soul". Girls' lives were closely controlled in college. The rules at Stockwell in London included: "Never go out alone; don't talk at dinner time; never speak after 10.10 p.m.; always wear a bonnet on a Sunday, never leave a square inch of dinner on your plate." They were to adopt "neatness and plainness of dress. No flowers, ornament or other finery should be worn." Most college learning was factual recitation: hundreds of lines of poetry; history facts "from a tiny 5d. book which contained strings of names and dates"; lists of capes, bays and rivers. By contrast, the remarkable Bishop Otter College in Chichester showed a quality and culture that made it a pioneer. Towards the end of the century, day training colleges attached to Universities helped supply better-quality teachers.

A school staff might consist of a certificated Head, an assistant or two, and some apprentice pupil-teachers. Women dominated the profession. Most teachers were extremely young; in 1870 about half were mere teenage apprentices. The pupil-teacher learned his craft by making mistakes, working long hours with large classes, spending evenings in study, and Saturdays in preparation. Pupil-teacher centres, established by large Boards in the 1880s, improved matters by allowing trainees to study half-time under special staff.

For the pupil, school life was grim. Discipline, given the nature of teacher and learners, was harsh. Movement was regimented. The cane was in constant use. "I never remember seeing my headmaster in school when he had not a cane hanging by the crook of his left wrist", wrote a pupil-teacher. Every blot, every spelling or sum error or defect of behaviour was given a number of "stripes". In such an atmosphere, pupils reacted with violence: bruised shins, even broken limbs, were reported among teachers.

The idea of compulsory schooling spread only gradually. The 1870 Act had empowered Boards to make bye-laws to make children attend school. London and other large cities compelled attendance for five- to ten-year-olds. Other districts, especially where

Boards had been enforced, were reluctant to follow. Lord Sandon's Act of 1876 set up school attendance committees, even in voluntary districts, and declared it was a parent's duty to see his child educated. Another Act of 1880 (A. J. Mundella's) forced all committees to make bye-laws. The state thus demanded that each child should attend school to the age of ten. Thereafter his schooling depended on the needs of his district: he could leave by passing the test of a certain standard, or with the so-called "Dunce's Certificate", by making a certain number of school attendances.

The machinery of compulsion was based on "visitors", the resented "School Board men". They went to the haunts of truant children—stations, markets, street Punch-and-Judy shows. Children were hidden; abuse and objects were hurled at the officials. Offending parents were summoned to the Board. Worst offenders were fined, although magistrates were often lenient, one commenting, "There are more important interests than education. People must live ..." Good attendance was rewarded. A good class might receive a banner; an individual a certificate or medal (one such was inscribed: "Delay not. Time Flies."). Some Boards ran fearful truant schools, like prisons, where boys were given manual labour, even suffering solitary confinement.

Attendance was hardest to enforce in the countryside, where child labour was still useful. Powerful squires or farmers could over-ride the law. A Devon teacher noted: "Sent to one farmer for six boys employed in mangel picking. Received a message to the effect—that when he wanted boys he would have them ..." Haymaking or harvest brought mass absences. Bird-scaring, gleaning, stone-gathering, or cottage industries kept poor children from school. A wet day was a menace for children who had no overcoats or sturdy boots. Frustrated teachers recorded other excuses for absence: "stopping to see the soldiers pass"; "to see steam ploughing machine at work"; "having been after the hounds".

Classwork in elementary schools was dominated, until the 1890s, by "payment by results". The Code, reconsidered each year by the Department, laid out the grant-earning requirements for the schools. Details were worked out by civil servants, the "examiners" of the Department, university graduates who knew nothing of the schools. Application of the Code was carried out by Her Majesty's Inspectors. Their role had changed drastically. Some had become petty tyrants hated by teachers. Runciman drew a picture of the worst type as "Mr. Puzzle H.M.I.": "He has never denied himself the luxury of small tyranny; he has never held back a cruel word or useless sneer."

Inspection day was a time for best clothes for teachers and pupils. "There was no singing or quarrelling on the way to school that morning", remembered Flora Thompson in *Lark Rise to Candleford* (1939). "The children, in clean pinafores and well-blackened boots, walked deep in thought or, with open spelling or table books in hand, tried to make up in an hour for all their wasted yesterdays." In his *Memoirs*, a Yorkshireman, Joseph Ashby, recalled "all the pupils and teachers would be listening until, at ten o'clock, a dog cart would be heard on the road ... In it would come two gentlemen with deportment of high authority with rich voices." Nerves infected pupils and teachers as the Inspector recorded test results in his ominous code: X (excellent), T (good pass), / (pass), O (failure). Stress forced some teachers into fraud. Test problems were passed from school to school. Secret signals (hands in pockets = multiply; hands behind back = subtract) told the pupils what to do. Pupils continued to "read" when they dropped the book or held it upside down. (As a counter-measure, Inspectors might ask pupils to read a passage backwards.)

Reading, writing and arithmetic were the basis of the test. Graded readers were prepared exhaustively. Standard I read single syllables: "The poor bird lay dead in its cage. It had died for want of food." Standard VI struggled over: "This property of gold of being capable of extension to so extraordinary a degree is owing to the great tenacity or cohesion of particles." Yet Flora Thompson recalled her "Royal Reader" with pleasure: "There was enough there to enthral any child." A Yorkshireman, Fred Kitchen, noted: "Life has been made richer because when ploughing up a nest of field mice, I could recite Robert Burns's 'Ode to a Field Mouse'. I learned of a world beyond. In fancy I got wrecked on Coral Island or shared the adventures of Robinson Crusoe." Writing began on slates (cleaned with spit and coat sleeve) and progressed to copy-books in which to practise copper-plate handwriting, a necessity in an age before typewriters. Even an H.M.I. asked: "Of what use can it be to copy—such crackjaw words as 'Zumiologist' or such pompous moral phrases as these—'Study moral rectitude', 'Wanton actions are very unseemly'." Mathematics was least successfully taught. Victorian teachers liked the elaborate problem to occupy the class, while

Inspectors favoured puzzle arithmetic. "What number, divided by 154, brings the quotient of 154 and the remainder 54?" was a Standard III test question in 1889.

Memorizing and passivity were features of the Code system. An Inspector lamented that he had never heard a child "ask a question of its teacher on the subject of the lesson." Nor was it efficient: only a quarter of four million scholars passed all their tests in 1880.

The curriculum was gradually widened. In 1871 grants were awarded in "specific subjects", more advanced work chosen from a list of approved courses for senior Standards. In 1875 "class subjects" were introduced (grammar, geography, history and needlework) intended for average classes above Standard I. Too often these subjects became recitation of facts; the towns of France (in alphabetical order) or railway stations on the London to Holyhead line were examples of "geography". One history teacher boasted that his pupils could "repeat names and dates of the Kings of England, very fast and correctly, backward from Queen Victoria." Object lessons qualified as "science". An Inspector described them as "the repetitions of a hideous dream—I see the fatal apparatus got ready ... and the picture card, or the object ... and I am told that the object is 'opaque' or 'tangible' or 'transparent' or what not ..." A new Code of 1882 added a Standard VII and awarded grants according to percentage success of all the school's pupils.

The increased demands of the Codes brought resentment from voluntary schools, who could not keep up with building requirements or teach new subjects. Conservative elements accused the Boards of "over-pressure" on children. In 1884 a doctor, Sir J. Crichton-Browne, declared that schooling was increasing mental disease in the young: "Since the recent spread of education, the increase of deaths from hydrocephalus (water on the brain) has not been among infants but among children over five years old." Tales were told of the child dying of brain fever, murmuring, "Father, I cannot do my sums." Mundella, the Vice-President of the Department, was asked in Parliament "if the number of children going to lunatic asylums had increased recently?" More enlightened opinion realized that schooling was indeed too much for half-starved city children.

The Council for promoting Penny Dinners, a voluntary group, began to provide simple meals in schools. The Department declined to help, pushing responsibility onto the family: "Many idle and improvident parents have been tempted to neglect their children ... in the hope that sympathy might be awakened, and their children fed at other people's expense."

The Cross Commission of 1888 considered progress in elementary schooling since 1870. This Report marked the beginning of a changed attitude. "Payment by results" was condemned as "a system of cram, which ... ought to be relaxed in the interests of the scholars, of the teachers and of education itself." In 1890, George Kekewich, Secretary of the Department, abolished the grants for the Three Rs and provided a fixed "capitation grant", based on average attendance at a school. He wished to promote "greater happiness in their work for both teachers and children", aiming "to substitute for the bald teaching of facts ... the development of interest and intelligence and the acquirement of real substantial knowledge." By 1897 even grants for tests in specific subjects disappeared. The grip of "payment by results" was loosened.

The 1890s accordingly saw important developments in the schools. There were more subjects: cookery, taught in well-equipped centres or travelling vans; wood and metal craft that "gave reality to much of the abstract teaching of the school"; physical education, beginning with drill and evolving into the elegant Swedish exercise system. In infant departments of London Board schools, "Kindergarten" lessons became common. These were based on the ideas of Friedrich Froebel (1782–1852), a German, who stressed the value of constructive play for the young child: "Play is the purest, most spiritual activity of man at this stage." "Kindergarten", a general theory of child learning intended to colour the whole school life of a child, was mistakenly applied as single lessons; nonetheless it led to better infant teaching. Runciman wrote of a Deptford school: "It seems as though love were in the very air." At the other end of school life, some Boards began grouping able pupils into Higher Grade schools, carrying studies beyond Standard VII (see Chapter 5). Progress towards free elementary education began in the 1890s. An Act of 1891 gave schools a grant of ten shillings (50p) a year to replace "school pence" of 3d (1p), a week, previously given by parents. Despite fears of future "free meals, free clothes, free everything", Parliament united to applaud the Act. It proved "a most conspicuous success", bringing "a great influx of children into our schools".

Such expansion brought renewed resentment from Conservative

elements. A letter in a Nottingham paper condemned "frivolous pursuits" in Board schools, declaring that people were employed to dirty plates for girls to wash. A letter to *Punch* attacked the aspirations of working-class pupils: "The boys all want to be clerks; what the girls want to be we are not informed, but domestic service is not to be thought of ... And for this have I paid trebled rates."

The declining condition of voluntary schools continued to cause concern. The matter became a political issue, Liberals favouring the Boards, Conservatives the Church schools. Demands for general reform grew. While the larger Boards had worked well, there were too many inefficient small Boards, especially in the countryside, where farmer members were often greedy for child labour. Sir John Gorst, Vice-President of the Education Department, said that "the School Boards in country districts ... represent the worst kind of local authority that could be devised." The cost of Board elections and the complexities of administration, where the Departments tried to correspond with all 2,568 Boards individually, were other factors in demands for reform. The new County Councils (set up after 1888) promised a more efficient administrative device. After complicated political activity (see Chapter 6) the Conservatives' 1902 Education Act dissolved the Boards and replaced them with Local Education Authorities. Thus the School Board era came to an end.

What were its achievements? A wider reading public was created allowing shrewd journalists to make fortunes in the 1880s and '90s. Earlier in the century there had been working-class papers (such as the Chartist *Northern Star* which sold 50,000 copies a week in 1839). Yet the years after 1870 produced the popular newspaper. George Newnes's pioneer periodical, *Tit-Bits*, founded in 1881, was aimed at "the great new generation that is being turned out by the Board schools ... who can just read, but are incapable of sustained attention. People of this kind want something to occupy them in trains, and on buses and trams." Alfred Harmsworth devised the simplified newspapers, the *Daily Mail* (1896) and the *Daily Mirror* (1904) for the same audience. For the children there were fascinating comics and "penny dreadfuls".

The broadly civilizing effect of the elementary schools was regarded with pride. That "great horde of street loafers who infest every large town", those "crowds of young savages" of mid-Victorian times were disappearing. H.M.I. King noted in 1895 "how roughness of manner has been soothed away, how readily and intelligently they can answer a question, how the half-hostile suspicion with which they regarded a stranger has disappeared ..." The sociologist Charles Booth, in his grim picture of poverty, *Life and Labour of the People of London*, published in the 1890s, wrote hopefully of the Board schools as "uniformly handsome, commodious, substantial and well-arranged ... the high water mark of the public conscience." Here he saw children who were "wholesome, bright-looking, well-fed, well-clad, eager for notice, smart, full of life." They seemed the products of worthy reform, portents of a brighter future world.

A wretched little creature, who, clutching at the rags of a pair of trousers with one of its claws ... pattered with bare feet over the muddy stones ... Fifty like it ... were about me in a moment, begging ... clamouring, yelling, shivering in their nakedness and hunger. The piece of money I had put into the claw of the child ... was clawed out of it ... and soon I had no notion in what part of the obscene scuffle in the mud, of rags and legs and arms and dirt, the money might be.

CHARLES DICKENS
On London's street children in *The Uncommercial Traveller* (1861)

I suppose it will be absolutely necessary to educate our masters ... From the moment you entrust the masses with power, their education becomes an imperative necessity.

ROBERT LOWE
Pamphlet on the Reform Act (1868)

What is our purpose in this Bill? Briefly this, to bring elementary education within the reach of every English home, aye and within the reach of those children who have no home ... Upon the speedy provision of elementary education depends our industrial prosperity ... The good, safe working of our constitutional system ... Upon this speedy provision depends also our national power.

W. E. FORSTER
Introduction of the Education Bill (1870)

They were a wild lot gathered in the Willow Alley shed ... Most of the little fellows had been used to blows ... Some were cowed and shy but vicious, and some were dulled into semi-imbecility by hunger, disease, ill-usage ... not one knew the entire alphabet and those who had picked up a slight idea of the letters from the street hoardings were decidedly vague. The teachers found it impossible to interest them in any subject for more than five minutes.

J. RUNCIMAN

On the first London Board pupils in *Schools and Scholars* (1887)

Sir,
*   The dark and deadly poison of infidelity is uprearing its rank growth in our midst ... An avowed atheist is preaching in one of our Board schools. Are we to be taxed that the faith for which Ridley and Latimer suffered may be crushed? Let us expel this cockatrice from our midst, sir, and let the flag of Britain fly unsullied in the breeze.*

Letter in a London paper

Quoted in J. Runciman *Schools and Scholars* (1887)

These solid, large-windowed blocks, which still rise everywhere above the slate roofs of mean suburbs, which meant for hundreds of thousands their first glimpse of a life of cleanliness, order, light and air ...

G. M. YOUNG

On London Board schools in *Victorian England* (1936)

Would you like to know the reason
Why we all look bright and gay
As we hasten to our places?
This is our Inspection Day!

You know we've done our duty,
Duly striving with our might.
Teacher says we need not worry
Though our sums will not come right.
So we are glad and gay
Though 'tis Inspection Day!

Elementary School song
Wiltshire (1880s)

While hewing yews, Hugh lost his ewe
And put it in the Hue and Cry ...
You brought the ewe back by and by
And only begged the hewer's ewer
Your hands to wash in water pure ...

Elementary school dictation exercise

How many furlongs, rods, yards, feet, inches and barley-corns will reach round the earth, supposing it according to best calculation to be 25,020 miles?

Sum set in a Suffolk village school (1890s)

Where are the 3 Rs now? No, the age of the 3 Rs is dead, buried and pulverized into invisible dust.

The Schoolmaster on the New Code (1891)

The school is a living thing, and should be judged as a living thing, not merely as a factory producing a certain modicum of examinable knowledge.

The end of "payment by results"
Report of Education Department (1898)

"Look at those big isolated clumps of buildings, rising above the slates, like brick islands in a lead-coloured sea."
"The Board Schools?"
"Light-houses, my boy! Beacons of the future. Capsules, with hundreds of bright little seeds in each, out of which will spring the wiser, better England of the future."

Sherlock Holmes to Dr. Watson
in SIR ARTHUR CONAN DOYLE's *The Naval Treaty* (1889)

i

iv

"THE EDUCATIONAL QUESTION."

THE SCHOOL (BOARD) MATCH.

EDUCATION'S FRANKENSTEIN—A DREAM OF THE FUTURE.

(*Dedicated to the School-Board.*)

ix

xi

xvi

4 The Golden Age of the public schools: 1860–1918

Despite the reforms of Thomas Arnold, criticism of the public schools flared up again in 1860. An anonymous correspondent, "Pater Familias", attacked Eton in *The Cornhill Magazine*. An expensive, narrow, ill-supervised education produced too many boys who needed extra coaching even to pass examinations for the Army or Civil Service. The school taught only "luxury and self-indulgence". The *Edinburgh Review* followed this attack by raising doubts about misuse of endowment funds, demanding that "enormous revenues willed for the promotion of education ... should not be illegally diverted ... into the pockets of a small number of individuals who are not entitled to them."

The Government could not ignore these suggestions of incompetence and corruption. In 1861 a Royal Commission, chaired by Lord Clarendon, was formed to examine the administration and curriculum of "The Nine" élite schools: Eton, Winchester, Harrow, Westminster, Charterhouse, Rugby, Shrewsbury, Merchant Taylors and St. Paul's. Its Report, published in 1864, presented a vivid picture of mid-Victorian school life and the educational attitudes of the time.

Certain public fears were calmed. There had been an improvement in "moral and religious training" in the schools. The prefect system was "admitted to have been most important in its effects on national character and social life." Boys were better cared for: therefore "the old roughness of manners has in a great measure disappeared, and, with it, the petty tyranny and thoughtless cruelty ... which used indeed to be thought inseparable from the life of a public school."

The curriculum was too narrow: "A young man is not well

educated if all his information is shut up within one narrow circle." The tedium of narrow classical studies allowed the schoolboy vice, "simple idleness", to flourish. Modern subjects should be introduced to balance traditional learning, as had been done in the Prussian "Gymnasia".

Practical management reforms were contained in the Public Schools Act of 1868. Restrictions imposed by ancient endowments were removed. Financial abuses were corrected by new governing bodies which included representatives of the Universities and learned societies (Eton's, for example, included a scientist from the Royal Society). There was to be no government inspection as this would "degrade the great public schools of England down to the level of village schools". After this mild breeze of change, the schools settled down to their "Golden Age", to forty years of prosperity and esteem.

The public school was a miniature world, what the Victorian commentator Charles Pascoe, called "a complete social body ... a society, in which we must not only learn but act and live." Its near-absolute ruler was the Headmaster, a bearded or whiskered patriarchal figure, who was manager of and spokesman for his school, and whose skill had a crucial effect on its fortunes. The rewards were considerable—the Heads of Eton, Harrow and Rugby at least were wealthy enough to aspire to the way of life of the gentry, and a successful man could expect a further career in the Church (four public school Heads became Archbishops of Canterbury). Competition for Headships was severe. Henry Butler sent in thirty-one testimonials for the Harrow post in 1859, while T. W. Jex-Blake submitted sixty-five, bound and printed as a book, for Haileybury in 1867. (He was not appointed.) The personalities of these "very superior men" made unforgettable impressions on their pupils. The archetype was B. H. Kennedy of Shrewsbury with "his tall and striking figure ... his bright, piercing eye, his mighty voice echoing among the rafters". Yet they had their well-loved eccentricities. Temple, of Rugby, liked climbing trees; Moss, of Shrewsbury, feigned ignorance of sport; Bradley, of Marlborough, loved wild cross-country horse rides.

The task of assistant masters was to teach classics. Their qualifications had to be acceptable to parents. They might be Old Boys and were graduates of Oxford or Cambridge (one Head spoke scathingly of products of "Dublin, London or a Scotch university").

House-masters were well rewarded and often received presents from parents, but other assistants were under-paid, postponing the luxury of marriage as they scrambled for promotion. They were rarely consulted and had to submit to the whims of the Head. Below the assistants in status were "extra masters" teaching mathematics, French, writing, science or music. Even mathematics masters could not wear a gown or take a House. Below them were the "professionals", sports coaches, who were to become increasingly important.

At the top of the schoolboy hierarchy were the prefects, given responsibility (including flogging powers) for discipline outside the classroom. Lowest in status were the fags, first-year boys who served the seniors. At Eton the cry "Come here", brought juniors running; last boy did the task. At Westminster, juniors watched the morning clock and called the time as their seniors lingered in bed. At Winchester, they battled to secure their master's breakfast, or miserably "kicked in" at football or "watched out" at cricket.

Schools were structured from Fourth Form to majestic Sixth Form. Sets were elaborately named and divided, from the simple alpha, beta, gamma, to "the Remove", "Shell" or "the Twenty", even, at Eton, "Sense" and "Nonsense". As knowledge was more important than chronological age, one set might contain several age groups—at Shrewsbury, a boy of ten sat down with a sixteen-year-old. A clever boy was rapidly promoted; a dunce was held back. In the great school-room, still common in early Victorian times, boys sat in groups around their masters, waiting to be called up to "construe" (recite in translation) the work set for preparation, while others studied their books. There was little expository class teaching. Composition of Latin or Greek verses was the most difficult task. An Eton boy remembered "the dismal confinement in the vitiated atmosphere; the oceans of ink in which we and our papers wallowed; the pitiful efforts with which a few verses were evolved as the result of two hours' labour; the fractiousness of pent-up boyhood." Only later in the century were classrooms and class teaching common.

Despite criticism of the classical curriculum, Latin and Greek continued to dominate public school studies. The ancient languages, commented the Clarendon Report, were a perfect "gymnastic" for the growing mind, grammar providing "logical accuracy of expression" for life, while literature—the "noblest poetry, the finest

eloquence, the deepest philosophy, the wisest historical writing"—
taught morality.

Yet the Clarendon Commission had been worried by the image of
the average public schoolboy "almost ignorant of geography and of
the history of his own country, unacquainted with any modern
language but his own" and "hardly competent to write English
correctly, to do a simple sum; a total stranger to the laws which
govern the physical world." To the men building an era of
tremendous technical advance, the last point seemed most
paradoxical. The eminent scientist, Michael Faraday, interviewed by
Lord Clarendon, was amazed that schools taught boys only "to
accept general ideas of a literary kind, and to say all the rest is
nonsense and belongs to the artisan." The crucial struggle to make
science a respectable subject was long and hard-fought.

Why were the public schools so conservative? Heads argued that
it was hard to find suitable masters, that laboratories were expensive,
that there were no textbooks, that parents were hostile to scientific
studies. Some schools were prepared to see science as a quaint
interest: both boys and masters had their geological collections or
went out botanizing. Voluntary lectures might be organized in the
summer term: optics, electricity, astronomy were favourite topics,
and each talk culminated in a dramatic experiment.

The influential *Essays on a Liberal Education* (1868), edited by
leading scientists, set out arguments showing the educative value of
science. This led to the production of better textbooks,
commissioned by the publishers, Macmillan, from leading scientists,
and to the establishment of "Modern Sides" for non-classical studies,
in some schools, notably Harrow. Yet the Devonshire Report (1875),
surveying English scientific education, still condemned public
school inertia: "Considering the increasing importance of science to
the material interests of the country, we cannot but regard its almost
total exclusion from the training of the upper and middle classes as
little less than a national misfortune."

Public school buildings, greatly extended during this "Golden
Age", were designed to impress: the grand façades and spacious
grounds echoed the country house or cathedral close in suggesting
the space and seclusion of the well-off. Tudor "collegiate" style
remained popular, though Victorian religious fervour produced the
pinnacles and pointed arches of the Gothic revival in schools with
Anglican links. Lancing's huge chapel, a Sussex landmark, was the

supreme example. By contrast, Prince Albert's favoured Wellington College was in plain "Queen Anne" style, to match its practical ambitions.

Within the buildings life was vigorous and harsh, enlivened by games and friendship, by curious tradition, and darkened by punishment. Living conditions were austere. The barrack-like dormitories, the walls scarred by pupils' names, were only gradually partitioned. Eton boys wildly hunted rats across Long Chamber and, at Westminster, rain beat through chinks in the lofty windows. Washing facilities were primitive: at Shrewsbury, even in the 1870s, boys ran naked to a backyard to "swill" water over each other. Later in the century, a doctor noted: "I have seen cesspools at one of the most popular and expensive schools ... in such a state of repletion that it would be impossible for the boys to use them without defiling themselves with the decomposing ordure." Outbreaks of serious illness were frequent, sometimes causing a school to move from its unhealthy site, as did Arnold's Rugby in 1841, or Uppingham in 1876.

The study was the centre of a boy's life at school. Charles Pascoe lovingly described the "little den ... the furniture consisting of a tiny sofa, chair, stool and table". The walls were decorated "with pictures, stuffed birds, stags' heads ... Nailed to the door, a horseshoe may be noticed." So small was the room that "often-times a boy, in his frantic haste, will drag the cloth off his table and so bring books, candles and spirit lamp in disastrous confusion to the floor." However there were "worse places in the world than a School House study, when you have drawn the curtains and lighted the candles." As school meals were so poor (Winchester boys were careful to avoid disturbing the sand mixed with the sugar in their tea) much amateur cooking took place in the studies.

Clarendon had defined the public schoolboy as "a high spirited English lad, who has the restless activity and love of play that belong to youth and health, who ... thinks somewhat slowly, and does not express himself readily and to whom mental effort is troublesome." Such boys carried on warfare with their masters. An Etonian recalled: "animals were frequently introduced; rats and mice might be seen to career about the boards of upper school; a dog was even introduced into chapel ... A favourite trick ... was to stretch a band of india-rubber all along a form and to twang it ... producing a noise which is most disconcerting." In return, punishment was fierce.

"Lines" were copied in copper-plate writing from classical texts. A single penalty was ten lines, but one Wellington boy gathered 1,500 in a week. Flogging was carried out with various implements—simple rods, split canes, birch bundles, weapons weighted with lead. At Eton, a boy knelt over the "block", trousers pulled down, while at Christ's Hospital the victim was spreadeagled over a man's back. Bodies were beaten raw, with birch fragments embedded in wounds. A final penalty was expulsion, dramatic for major offences, or unspectacular at term end for inadequate scholars.

A complex tangle of "boy custom"—unwritten school rules and customs—was required learning for new boys. At Harrow, the football eleven, in red dressing gowns, stood juniors on a table before them for examination on the game. "What is the last letter but fifteen in the rules?" and "How many nails are allowed in boots?" were characteristic questions. Failure brought "progging" with toasting forks or a glass of salt water. Charles Pascoe collected a glossary of schoolboy slang. Here are some bizarre examples:

Brum (Winchester): stingy, penniless.
Cheesy (Charterhouse): good, excellent.
Croppled (Winchester): unable to recite a lesson.
Froust (Harrow): extra sleep on Sunday.
Scug (Eton): an untidy or dirty boy.
Swaggerman (Shrewsbury): a boy good at everything.

There were traditional occasions. Eton's "Montem" had been most spectacular, until rioting ended it in 1844. Eton boys had paraded Windsor streets in fancy dress, extorting "salt" (money) from watching crowds, the collected funds being given to the school captain. The "Royal Shrewsbury Hunt" was a cross-country run performed with the ritual of a hunt, led by a huntsman in "black velvet cap decorated with golden whips". At Charterhouse, there was the Lemon Peel Fight between "Boarders" and "Gownboys", a survival of the medieval school festival, using half-lemons left from dinner.

The model for a more civilized school community was provided by Edward Thring (1821–87) at Uppingham. Thring had suffered in the Long Chamber at Eton. He considered that better organization ("machinery", as he called it) and buildings and equipment ("mechanical improvement") could transform the public schools. Four hundred boys were carefully divided into a dozen Houses, and into classes of thirty. Thring thought every boy was good for something, and a wide curriculum gave each his chance. There were gardens, craft shops, a swimming pool and England's first proper school gymnasium. A fine musical tradition began, with half the boys playing instruments. Parents flocked to send their sons to such a practical, caring school.

Thring's reforms anticipated the elaborate time-tabling and organization—marked by school clubs, badges, uniforms and colours—that changed the public schools of the 1870s and '80s. The old "boy republics" were gradually undermined.

In the last decades of the century, the cult for sport came to dominate the schools. Shrewd Heads used boys' love of games to absorb their spare time and energies.

Early in the century, games were loosely organized and very rough. In "football in cloister" at Charterhouse, scrimmages lasted three-quarters of an hour, during which "shins would be kicked black and blue; jackets and other articles of clothing almost torn into shreds". Rugby boys wore iron-tipped boots, called "navvies", "the profile of which at the toe much resembled the ram of an ironclad". At Winchester, fags stood, legs apart, as living goal posts. There were no defined teams, and crowds of boys took part.

The first written codes of rules (such as "The laws of football as played at Rugby school" of 1845) advanced skill beyond brute strength, and the network of inter-school matches, with opponents chosen with nice regard to status, was established by the 1860s. Schools began hiring professional coaches: John Lillywhite, the famous cricketer, joined Rugby in 1850, and by 1854, the school "Twenty" was proudly playing "An England XI". The tokens of sporting success became highly valued. Boys at Rugby coveted the "velvet skull cap with gold or silver tassel ... acquiring value with shabbiness", that imposed on its owner "a certain obligation to live decently before his fellows, and to observe all the punctilios of good form."

Marlborough was a striking example of the power of the games cult. The violence of the school's first years ended with the appointment of G. E. L. Cotton as Head in 1852. Well-organized sport drew boys away from their hunting and poaching. In Chapel, Cotton preached the idea of "the whole man", combining "intellectual and bodily excellence". Other theorists came to defend the educational value of games, which the writer Charles Kingsley defined as "temper, self-restraint, fairness, honour ... and all that 'give and take' of the life which stands a man in such good stead when he goes forth into the world." The phrase "muscular Christianity" became a formula for public school education, combining the benefits of the playing field with the lingering spirit of Arnold.

As the tide of Imperialism rose in late Victorian England, loyalty to team and school blended easily into patriotism and service to Queen and Empire. The competitor of the playing field became the frontiersman, working to maintain and extend the boundaries of Empire. Old Boys' articles in *The Marlburian* reflect this: "Fire in Tasmania"; "Pleasures of the Veldt", "With the attacking force in the Khyber". The public schoolboy, fit and dutiful, used to responsibility, seemed the perfect agent of Empire.

Yet athleticism bred a dangerous contempt for the "clever" boy. This philistinism and the need to conform to the "manly" image, caused stress in more sensitive, introverted boys. In the vogue for public school memoirs following the Great War, they expressed their resentment. The artist Roger Fry was in "sullen revolt" against Clifton, where terms passed "heavily, respectably, monotonously". The poet Robert Graves described the dreadful bullying at Charterhouse before 1914 in *Goodbye to All That* (1929).

By contrast, popular writers, in stories for boys, created powerful propaganda for public school life. Dean Farrar's *Eric or Little by Little*, Kipling's *Stalky and Co*, Talbot Baines Reed's *Fifth Form at St. Dominic's* followed *Tom Brown's Schooldays* in presenting the atmosphere of the school community. The Billy Bunter stories, in the Edwardian comics, *Magnet* and *Gem*, described the glamour of "the old school" to working-class boys. The Etonian, George Orwell, amusingly mocked these fantasies in his essay on "Boys' Weeklies" (1940): "Outside the wind is whistling, the ivy clusters thickly round the old grey stones ... We are all settling down to a tremendous tea of sausages, sardines, crumpets ... After ten we shall sit round the study fire—discussing the team for next week's match against Rookwood. Everything is safe, solid and unquestionable ..."

Early twentieth century militarism was reflected in public school cadet corps. Links with the services had always been strong, especially at Wellington or Cheltenham. When the Volunteer Corps was created in 1858, many schools set up units. The crisis of the Boer War led to an outcry for military reform. Pressure groups, such as the National Service or Navy Leagues, favoured conscription.

Lord Roberts, hero of the war in South Africa, toured schools campaigning. The Army reforms of 1908 produced the Officers' Training Corps (O.T.C.) intended to provide young soldiers ready for war, from the public schools and universities. Schools were enthusiastic: corps was time-tabled, and boys enlisted en masse. They drilled and marched, sang round the fire at the annual camp at Aldershot, many of them doomed to die in the carnage of the Great War of 1914–18.

The casualty rate among junior officers was high. Public school war memorials therefore displayed long lists of names: from Rugby, 686 Old Boys died; from Malvern 457 of the 2,800 that served. One third of all Haileybury entrants between 1905 and 1912 fell at the Front. Young men wrote their Roman farewells to the old school from the trenches, displaying their Imperial ideas and dogged courage. A former Dulwich pupil, Paul Jones, killed in 1917, wrote typically: "It is the chief virtue of the public school system that it teaches one to make sacrifices willingly for the sake of *esprit de corps*. Well, clearly, if the public school men hold back, the others will not follow." Those enormous memorials commemorated not merely the fallen but the end of a particular educational ideal.

No Latin or Greek may make Master Jacky a dull boy; but Latin and Greek without anything else go far towards making Master Jacky a very dullard. Parents are beginning to feel this, and to ask whether a skinful of classical knowledge, with a little birching thrown in for nothing, be an equivalent for the two hundred a year they pay for the education of a boy at Eton.

The Illustrated London News (1861)

The English people are indebted to these schools for the qualities on which they pique themselves most—for their capacity to govern others and control themselves, their aptitude in combining freedom with order. Their public spirit, their vigour and manliness of character ... their love of healthy sports and exercise. These schools have been the chief nurseries of our statesmen ... and they have had perhaps the largest share in moulding the character of an English gentleman.

The Clarendon Report (1864)

The time devoted at our schools, whether public or private, to Latin and Greek, is a Laputism [eccentricity] on which our great grand-children will look back, I believe, as we do to the witch mania.

CHARLES KINGSLEY
Letter (1859)

That the natural knowledge which has been given the world in such abundance during the last fifty years ... should remain untouched, and that no sufficient attempts should be made to convey it to the young ... is to me a matter so strange that I find it difficult to understand.

MICHAEL FARADAY
in the Clarendon Report (1864)

Every boy is good for something. If he can't write iambics or excel in Latin prose, he has at least eyes and hands and ears. Turn him into the carpenter's shop, make him a botanist or a chemist, encourage him to express himself in music, and, if he fails all round, here at least he shall learn to read in public his mother tongue and write thoughtfully an English essay.

EDWARD THRING
On work at Uppingham in *Theory and Practice of Teaching* (1883)

> *One athletic rage*
> *Has seized Marlburians of every age.*
> *Now filled with frenzy, cricket all will play;*
> *Now, all absorbing football rules the day.*
> *Where'er you go, the topic is the same,*
> *And all our talk at table is "the game" ...*

The Marlburian (1876)

> *There's a breathless hush in the Close tonight—*
> *Ten to make and the match to win—*
> *A bumping pitch and a blinding light,*
> *An hour to play and the last man in.*
> *And it's not for the sake of a ribboned coat,*
> *Or the selfish hope of a season's fame,*
> *But his captain's hand on his shoulder smote:*
> *"Play up! Play up! and play the Game!"*

HENRY NEWBOLT
from *Vitai Lampada* (1908)

I look to you public schoolboys to set an example. Let it be your ambition to render yourself capable of becoming leaders of those others who have not your advantages should you ever be called upon to fight for your country ... Public school training inculcates just those qualities which are required in leaders of men ...

LORD ROBERTS
Speech (1906)

Good was his name; he played the Game,
And he made the red ball hum,
A King beloved as he stood and shoved
Or burst through the reeking scrum.
Farewell, young King, away you fling,
All in the flush of youth,
Playing the game, the grand last game
For England and for truth ...

Memorial poem to Capt. R. Langden
The Marlburian (December, 1916)

5   Secondary education in the late nineteenth century

The Taunton Report, 1868

The Clarendon Report had dealt with the major public schools. In 1864, the Schools Inquiry Commission, chaired by Baron Taunton, was appointed to consider other middle-class education: eight hundred endowed schools were examined, private schooling looked at and attention given to "the much neglected subject of female education".

The Taunton Report was published in 1868. The new proprietary foundations were praised: "Some of them rank with the most famous of the grammar schools ... there have not been anywhere more successful or more promising undertakings than these great modern schools." There were some good grammar schools, like those in York, Leeds and Doncaster: "All are under the care of accomplished and energetic men, are increasing in numbers, and are obtaining distinction at the Universities." Yet there were too many corrupt endowed schools. At Thame, two men shared £300 and taught only one pupil. Whitgift's Hospital, Croydon, endowed with £500 per annum, had had no pupils for thirty years. There were odd situations. In one school, fee-payers were divided from free scholars by a wooden partition, straddled by an elevated master's desk. "Unless he kept the two classes of pupil habitually apart", claimed the master, "the more respectable parents would object to pay ... Even in the playground there was no intercourse between them." The curriculum was often absurd. The Latin teaching ordained by the endowment often "literally comes to nothing". Other subjects were paid for as extras. "I have seen a class of children", wrote H.M.I. Fitch, "painfully employed in reading all day, and wholly unable to use a pencil or pen because their parents did not choose to pay the writing fee." The Report summed up: "Of the fact of the general decadence (of the grammar schools) there can be no doubt. The schools are not popular; they do not possess the confidence of parents." Private schooling was equally poor.

Commissioners were sent abroad to America and Europe. Matthew Arnold's description of Prussian High Schools caused great interest: "The Prussian system appears to be at once the most complete and the most perfectly adapted to its people of all that now exist." It was taken as a model for the Report's practical proposals. The country should be divided into eleven districts, each with a local education authority, presided over by a Minister of Education. Each district should be surveyed for need and three grades of secondary school provided to "correspond roughly ... to the gradations of society". The first would teach sons of professional men up to nineteen; the second, sons of "gentry of straightened means" up to sixteen; the third, sons of "tenant farmers ... small tradesmen, the superior artisan" up to fourteen. The last of these was "the most urgent educational need of the country". The first-grade school would follow a classical curriculum; the others more practical studies. Examinations by local inspectors would be "the pivot of all improvements".

The Endowed Schools Act of 1869 ignored these suggestions, which ran ahead of public opinion. Conservatism and class jealousy destroyed this proposed secondary school system. Individual schools, fearful of government intervention, clustered together, under the leadership of Edward Thring, to form the powerful Headmasters' Conference to protect their interests.

However, the Endowed School (later the Charity) Commission was given powers to reform existing schools, strong enough, it was said, "to convert a boys' school in Northumberland into a girls' school in Cornwall". Corruption and neglect were ended by schemes drawn up with school governors. By 1884, 595 new schemes had been accepted. Schools were transformed. Bradford Grammar School, existing in "general languor and feebleness" in 1868, became a dynamic institution in the years 1883–93, sending 108 boys to university and claiming 73 scholarships. Thus the old scandals of the grammar schools gradually disappeared. Yet opportunity for secondary schooling remained unsatisfactory, as the endowments corresponded to the distribution of wealth and populations of Medieval and Tudor England, not to the industrialized community. For example, an H.M.I. noted in 1895 that Manchester Grammar School, with 1,200 places, was serving a local population of five or six millions. In the last years of the century, various other agencies arose to provide a kind of secondary education.

Higher Grades, South Kensington and whiskey money

In the 1880s state elementary schooling began to evolve its own advanced education. The Taunton Report suggested this: "It might often be desirable to attach the schools of the third grade to the present elementary schools ... to admit ... children of labourers ... who seemed to deserve a longer and better education ... Sometimes a third-grade school might in this way be fed by several elementary schools". The expansion of the elementary curriculum and addition of Standard VII in 1882 led to the growth of "Higher Tops" (advanced classes within a school) or "Higher Grade" schools, which creamed able children from a district. Sheffield was first with a Higher Central School in 1880, and other northern cities followed. There was a remarkable Seventh Standard school in Birmingham, and another in Deansgate, Manchester. Both had a typically scientific bias, the Birmingham school teaching only machine construction, chemistry and electricity. Although classes were over-large, morale was good. An official Report of 1895 described Leeds Higher Grade School as "the most interesting in Leeds in many ways, representing as it does the entering of a new power into the existing system of secondary education." The Headmaster saw his school as a force "passing with great strides across the realms of secondary education (which) may soon be battering at the doors of the ancient universities themselves." By 1895, there were sixty-seven such schools, acting as the growth points of the state school system.

Their existence was made possible by grants from the Department of Science and Art, which supplemented Board funds from rates and from Whitehall. This Department—"South Kensington" as it was called after its headquarters—started in 1837 as patron of industrial design. It had blossomed after 1859, when it was given powers to examine many scientific subjects, awarding certificates and grants to successful students and their teachers, in a blunt policy of "payment by results". The 1870 Science and Art courses attracted thousands of candidates from all kinds of class and institution. Much unintelligent cramming went on. Teachers swotted up the specially-written textbooks and passed information to pupils. Little practical work was done. Certificates could be collected by the dozen. Thus it was said that the highest number of agriculture awards was won by Londoners from Whitechapel, who never saw the countryside. The wonderful opportunity provided by the grants was well illustrated by the career of H. G. Wells. He was swept from life as a draper's assistant to study science in London under Professor T. H. Huxley, as a result of Science and Art examination successes won while he worked as a pupil-teacher at Midhurst Grammar School.

"Organized Science Schools" where pupils studied a planned two or three-year programme, proved most profitable grant earners. Half the Higher Grade schools were so established, and many endowed grammars benefited too. There were criticisms of the methods employed, however. Arthur Acland's *Studies in Secondary Education* (1892) took the Liverpool Institute as an example of bad practice. In dark, insanitary buildings, boys worked an eight-hour day, studying unconnected subjects, learned parrot fashion. Sturdy elementary schoolboys became "ill-formed, narrow-shouldered, stooping and suffering from weak eye-sight." Badly-paid teachers drove their pupils fiercely to earn themselves extra money.

"Whiskey money" provided another financial source for advanced schooling. A Royal Commission of 1884 on technical instruction (set up in the shadow of foreign competition) had demanded more secondary schooling as a basis for industrial training. An Act of 1889 gave the County and County Borough Councils (set up under the Local Government Act of 1888) power to raise a penny rate to found schools and provide scholarships. The strange accident of "Whiskey money" gave Councils extra funds for the same purposes. In 1890, the Government reduced the number of public houses. An extra tax on spirits had been intended to compensate publicans. Temperance interests persuaded Parliament to give these tax receipts (£800,000 in the first year) to County Councils to help with technical education. Thereafter, "Whiskey money" became a permanent government grant. Most remarkable of the activity it unleashed was that of London County Council's Technical Education Committee. Its Chairman, the Fabian socialist, Sidney Webb (1859–1947) interpreted "technical instruction" to mean any subject that provided "fitness for life", and the grants were accordingly given to "anything under the sun except Ancient

Greek and Theology". Webb's Committee thus created an elaborate network of scholarships to allow even the elementary schoolboy to climb the "educational ladder" to university.

Besides these public efforts at provision of post-elementary schooling, there were still hundreds of private establishments, offering cheap, pretentious education to lower-middle-class parents. The socialist, J. W. Martin, wrote (in a Fabian Tract of 1895) of "private, irregular enterprise ... They put mysterious letters after their names ... They issue delusive prospectuses; they lure shabby-genteel people into their parlours, and the thing is done." In *Kipps* (1905), H. G. Wells described such a school as "Cavendish Academy". A pupil's life consisted of "sitting on creaking forms, bored and idle, of blot licking and the taste of ink ... of the slimy surface of the laboured slates (and) dreary walks when the boys marched two by two, all dressed in the mortar-board caps that so impressed the widowed mothers."

All these various opportunities, in needless competition, produced confusion and waste. Reformers looked enviously at secondary systems abroad, especially in Germany. Matthew Arnold's pessimistic words to Taunton still rang true: "Our middle classes are among the worst educated in the world ... and our body of secondary schools the most imperfect and unserviceable in civilized Europe." In face of this muddle, a Royal Commission, chaired by James Bryce, was appointed in 1894 to examine possible reforms. One provision of the Bryce Report of 1895 was put into effect. An Act of 1899 created a Board of Education, controlled by a President and Parliamentary secretary, "to replace the competing agencies"— the Education Department, Charity Commission, and Department of Science and Art. A second provision was not accepted. The Report suggested that Local Education Authorities, formed by County Councils, should control secondary schools. Progress here became entangled with the struggle of Church and School Boards in elementary schooling. Reformers worked patiently on both issues to prepare the major legislation of 1902, that reconstructed both elementary and secondary education in England (see Chapter 6).

Experiment in secondary schooling
Dissatisfaction with conventional curriculum and structure produced some remarkable experiments in late nineteenth century secondary schools.

Abbotsholme in Derbyshire (1889) was the first of the so-called "progressive schools". It was founded by Cecil Reddie (1858–1932) partly under the inspiration of his friend, the socialist Edward Carpenter (who dreamed of regenerating England by a return to a simple life close to nature) and partly under the influence of the "method, clearness, organization" that he had seen in Germany. Abbotsholme was to be "an ideal, miniature Kingdom", first of many proposed "New Schools" from which sons of the "Directing Classes" would go out to rule a revitalized British Empire.

Reddie stressed a balanced curriculum and good health. Boys slept under rough blankets with all windows open before rising to a cold bath and morning run. They wore simple "rational-dress" clothes. Classwork was matched by daily manual work in the extensive gardens where boys tasted "the open air, the hardiness of sun and wind" and grew their own excellent food. Haymaking was the highlight of such outdoor activity, a symbolic lesson to show "the link between God and Nature". Co-operation, rather than competition, was stressed. Each boy's progress "upwards and outwards" towards an ideal of manhood was recorded on minutely-detailed reports decorated with the Union Jack.

Reddie's eccentricity almost ruined his school, but his ideas were spread abroad, especially to Germany, where a flourishing "Landschule" movement grew up. In England, a fruitful variant of the "New School" was Bedales (1893) set up by an assistant of Reddie, J. H. Badley. The same principles were employed with one major addition: co-education. A mixture of boys and girls, common in elementary schools, was almost unknown in the private sector. Badley, one of the wisest of English educationists, defended the mixed school: "We need a truer and happier relationship to take the place of the alternate phases of mutual contempt and mutual idolization that are encouraged by separate upbringing ... If the boy needs civilizing by the girl, no less ... is the girl's nature made fuller and more human by daily contact with the boy." The humane atmosphere and Badley's shrewd adoption of successful teaching ideas allowed Bedales to flourish, where Abbotsholme remained trapped in the "advanced thought" of the 1890s.

There were experiments with teaching method in more conventional grammar and public schools. F. W. Sanderson, Headmaster of Oundle from 1892, revitalized a declining school. "Education must be fitted to the boy; not the boy to education", was his theme. Creative work should replace passive learning. Classrooms were "tool sharpening rooms", where basic learning was acquired, which was then applied in projects in laboratory, workshop, library and art room. The large workshops for wood and metal-craft were the most striking of Sanderson's ventures. Here boys spent a week at a time, following a project from drawing board to finished article. (So skilled did boys become that they helped make munitions in the Great War.) Sanderson, described by H. G. Wells as "The Great Schoolmaster", was perhaps the first public school Head to take science seriously.

The Perse School in Cambridge saw many experiments in teaching method under the Headship of William Rouse, from 1902 to 1928. Besides "direct method" teaching of French and even Latin, novel English teaching was carried on by H. Caldwell-Cook, who described his work in *The Play Way* (1917). A child's delight in imaginative play was used to motivate him: island maps and model towns were prepared as a basis for written work. Above all there was the "Mummery", a tiny theatre workshop where boys acted out Shakespeare. Such inspired teaching made learning a pleasure. Rouse summed up: "No less work is done in a Morris dance than on a treadmill but it has a different effect on the human spirit."

Girls' education: the middle-class revolution
Better schooling for middle-class girls was part of the broad movement towards female emancipation.

The problem of governesses began the revolution. In 1843 the Governesses' Benevolent Institution was founded in London to help poor or aged women teachers. Pathetic hordes of women besieged the building. Its founders, the Rev. David Laing and the Christian Socialist, F. D. Maurice, wanted better education so that women could claim higher salaries. Tests for their teaching diploma revealed that most aspiring governesses were "the most pitiable of all victims of ignorance." From 1847, lectures were given by the Institution. So successful were these that it became Queen's College in 1848, having attracted royal support. Academic courses were open to governesses and "ladies" over the age of twelve, provided they were chaperoned at lectures by "lady visitors". In 1849, Bedford College was endowed by a rich widow as a non-denominational contrast to Anglican Queen's. Both colleges were, in effect, good secondary schools. Both had to endure press ridicule. Yet both attracted intelligent young women and were thus cradles for the movement to emancipate women.

Among the first pupils at Queen's were Frances Buss (1826–94) and Dorothea Beale (1831–1906), two great pioneers of girls' education. Frances Buss had begun her own tiny school for young ladies at eighteen. After Queen's had "opened a new life to me", she started, in 1850, a more ambitious venture, the North London Collegiate School for Ladies in Camden. As her family helped with teaching, the school, which taught 115 children by the end of its first year, had a homely atmosphere: Miss Buss was fond of "motherly hugs" and "loving words of praise", and kissed each pupil at dismissal. Yet it was startlingly democratic with no barriers to class or religious belief. "All pupils who enter are considered as upon the same equality", claimed Miss Buss. Daughters of tradesmen studied beside those of professional men; Jews and Catholics, in an age of discrimination, were easily accepted. Competitive study brought good results. The school's reputation grew. A description in 1872 caught its atmosphere: after passing the boards showing the names of scholarship winners, the visitor entered "a most attractive school room ... The bright young girls are arranged at long reversible desks ... (There is) an air of brightness and refinement to the whole room ... The long passages give them a convenient space for the musical gymnastics which form part of every day's work ..." Miss Buss's school became the pattern for the many girls' High Schools that sprang up later.

Dorothea Beale became Principal of the Ladies' College, Cheltenham in 1858. The founders of this proprietary school, opened in 1854 for "daughters and young children of noblemen and gentlemen", were determinedly in favour of "the cultivation of women's minds". Yet Miss Beale began her half-century reign amid a storm of complaints from conservative parents, who disliked an advanced curriculum that neglected the accomplishments, fearing that their girls "would be turned into boys". Such parents thought arithmetic "unladylike"; that Shakespeare was less valuable for a girl than "to be able to sit down at a piano and amuse her friends". Miss Beale's integrity and devotion gradually won the community round. Pupils remembered "the quiet face with its look of intense thoughtfulness ... the intellectual brow, the wonderful eyes with ... their expression of inner vision." The school was conducted in silence. No girl might speak to another in school hours, except during a morning conversation break. There were no physical punishments, only earnest appeals to a girl's better nature. Confidence in the school rose. The curriculum was widened to include science, Latin and Greek. In 1864 the first boarding house opened.

A third pioneer was Emily Davies (1830–1921), a determined reformer who linked girls' schooling to the rising feminist movement. She made the examination her first target for action. Women could not enter higher education without qualifications given by the Oxford and Cambridge Local Examinations started in 1858. Cambridge was sympathetic to Miss Davies's plea that girls should be allowed to enter. In 1863, eighty-three girls sat the tests at senior and junior level. Although most of them fared poorly in arithmetic, results were encouraging, and girls did not collapse with "brain fever" as pessimists had predicted. The experiment aroused public debate. The *Saturday Review* noted that "there is a strong and ineradicable male instinct that a learned ... young woman is one of the most intolerable monsters in creation." On the other side, Emily Davies spoke of the "almost complete mental blankness" of the middle-class woman's life. "All we claim", she concluded, "is that the intelligence of women shall have full and free development." In 1867 Cambridge opened its examinations to girls on a permanent basis.

The three pioneers all gave evidence to the Taunton Commission, insisting that reformed endowments should be used to help girls as well as boys. Commissioners' visits to old-fashioned girls' schools revealed a depressing inadequacy: there was too much pointless rote-learning; there were too many poor textbooks (especially the "noxious brood of catechisms"). The urgent need for better-qualified teachers was enough to sway the Commission: the Act of 1869 declared that "provision shall be made ... for extending to girls the benefits of endowments." Whereas there were only twelve endowed schools for girls in 1864, there were eighty by 1890. The 1869 Act has been called "the Magna Carta of Girls' education, the first acknowledgement by the state of their claim to a liberal education."

Progress was not swift enough for some reformers. The Women's Education Union was formed in 1871 from energetic women led by Maria Grey and her sister, Emily Sheriff. They intended "to win for women the right and means to the highest culture of which their nature is capable." A Girls' Public Day School Trust was launched in 1872: a fund, raised by selling shares, would be used to found and maintain efficient, inexpensive schools. The first opened in Chelsea in 1873 and, by 1891, the Trust controlled thirty-six schools. They imitated the academic standards and cheerful mingling of social classes of Miss Buss's school: "the gentleman's daughter ... follows a teacher's demonstration on the same board which is gazed at also by the children of the small shopkeeper." The G.P.D.S.T. schools had a powerful impact. They had "a larger influence on the improvement of feminine education than any single measure", wrote H.M.I. Fitch in 1890.

There were also girls' public schools: Roedean was founded in Brighton in 1885, and Wycombe Abbey in 1896. Although Miss Beale's influence was apparent, the model of boys' schools was more potent. The House system, prefects, organized games were important elements in their life. Roedean promised that "from two to three hours" daily would be allotted to outdoor exercise, reflecting the public school games cult of the 1880s.

The Bryce Commission of 1894 commended the spread of girls' schooling: "The idea that a girl, like a boy, may be fitted by education to earn a livelihood, or ... to be a more useful member of society, has become more widely diffused." The next problem was to extend secondary schooling for clever girls of "the industrial classes", giving them a chance to climb "the scholarship ladder". The 1902 Act was to provide such opportunity.

In Prussia the education department is simply the instrument which the people use to procure the fulfilment of their own desires. The Prussians believe in culture ... the result is an unrivalled body of teachers, schools meeting every possible need of every class, and a highly cultivated people.

The Taunton Report (1868)

It is impossible to convey in a report the impression which this school makes upon one of efficiency, energy and vitality ... No one ... can fail to realise that we are here in the presence of a new educational force, which has already developed to a vigorous and lusty youth (and) represents a new educational movement from below.

The Bryce Report (1895)
Comment on Leeds Higher Grade School.

... dispersed and unconnected forces, needless competition between the different agencies, and a frequent overlapping of effort, with much consequent waste of money, of time and of labour ...

The Bryce Report (1895)
Comment on confusion in secondary schooling

If it accomplishes its aim, the New School might well be called "La Giocosa", as being a place full of active and joyous life.

J. H. BADLEY
Bedales (1924)

The school should be a place where a boy comes not to learn but to create. Mathematics, languages and the elements of science are not ends, but tools, and these tools a boy must accustom himself to use ...
... Schools should be miniature copies of the world we should love to have.

F. W. SANDERSON
On work at Oundle School in *Sanderson of Oundle* (1924)

The picture brought before us of the state of middle-class female education is unfavourable ... want of thoroughness and foundation; want of system; slovenliness and showy superficiality; inattention to rudiments; undue time given to accomplishments ... want of organization—these may sufficiently indicate the character of the complaints we have received.

The Taunton Report (1868)
Comment on girls' education

6   English schooling in the twentieth century

The 1902 Education Act and after

In face of confusion in English education in the 1890s, "collectivists" from various political parties emerged in public debate. Important among them were Fabian socialists, led by Sidney Webb, who campaigned for a planned, efficiently administered society. They prepared well-researched, forcefully written "tracts" on many topics, including education.

The Bryce Report of 1895 had suggested a "collectivist" reorganization of education. A Bill of 1896, prepared by Sir John Gorst (1835–1911), Vice-President of the Education Department, proposed Local Authorities to control all schools in their areas. It was defeated by supporters of the School Boards— Liberals and socialists who admired their "primal democracy", and non-conformists, who resented the threatened "Tory-clerical" plan to give rate-aid to church schools.

Gorst worked on to undermine the Boards, so opening the way for a general restructuring of education. He was assisted by the remarkable Robert Morant (1863–1920), a civil servant in the Education Department, and another advocate of "national efficiency". In a complicated intrigue, they aimed to show that the Higher Grade schools, pride of the Boards, were technically illegal. Following a hint from Morant, the London Board's expenditure on Higher Grade schooling and evening classes was challenged by a government auditor, T. B. Cockerton, who claimed that rates could only be spent on elementary education. The High Court upheld this "Cockerton Judgement" in 1900. This was followed by regulations that severely limited the Board's work in the secondary sphere.

With the Boards thus discredited, comprehensive reform was

now possible. Sidney Webb caught the mood of the hour in the influential Fabian tract, *The Education Muddle and the Way Out* (1901): "What the national well-being demands is that every child, dull or clever, rich or poor, should receive all the education requisite for the full development of its faculties. For every child, in every part of the country, at least a 'national minimum' of education must be compulsorily provided." It was in this spirit that the 1902 Education Act was planned.

The Bill was introduced in the Commons in March, 1902, by Arthur Balfour (1848–1930), nephew of the Conservative leader, Lord Salisbury, whom he was to succeed as Prime Minister in July of the same year. Balfour had been persuaded that education was a vital political issue by Morant, who helped draw up the Bill.

The Act of December 1902 fundamentally changed the structure of English education. The School Boards were abolished. Instead, County and Borough Councils were constituted as Local Education Authorities (L.E.A.s), that took over all the legal powers of the Boards. They were to survey deficiencies in their districts. In particular, they were to build new council secondary grammar schools; co-ordinate local educational opportunities; help train teachers, and provide scholarships to make "a ladder from the elementary school to the university".

There was some compromise as a gesture to the Boards, lamented as "the best, the most fruitful and most beneficial educational agencies" by the Liberal opposition. So, a small "Part III Authority", heir of the Board in certain town districts, would run elementary schools, while a larger enclosing "Part II Authority" looked after secondary schools. Thus Harrogate became a "Part III", while the West Riding of Yorkshire, a "Part II" centred at Wakefield, administered Harrogate Grammar School, and the Technical and Art School. This clumsiness did not suit Morant, with his slogan "one education authority, and that to be paramount."

The L.E.A.s were also able to help voluntary schools of the various churches with their finances. Such schools were now called "non-provided": the church paid for building and up-keep, while the Authority paid running costs and teachers' salaries. (By contrast, other schools were "provided", that is, built and maintained by the local authority.) Authority nominees were to help manage church schools and overlook secular instruction. In this way, the poverty of the voluntary sector was ended, even if the "dual system" lingered on. This part of the Act caused fierce controversy for years. David Lloyd-George, the rising Liberal star, spoke against "Rome on the rates"—the grant of public funds to Catholic schools—while the non-conformist minister, John Clifford, told his followers to refuse to pay their rates. This final outburst of the old "religious difficulty" gradually faded as the merits of the reformed system became apparent.

The Act, which ended confusion, was followed by a decade of strenuous activity by Morant, Permanent Secretary of the Board of Education from 1902. His political masters became shadows beside this unique reformer, "a giant with a large pale face, and glowing eyes set in deep hollows". With his passion for work, he was, wrote the historian E. J. R. Eaglesham, "less of an administrator than an educational buccaneer, a desk-bound Francis Drake." A series of memoranda, inspired by Morant, flowed from the Board, shaping the system and guiding school life.

The abolition of "payment by results" had meant a certain loss of direction in the elementary sector. The Code of 1904 redefined these aims: "a sense of discipline, which should pervade the school" would "implant in the children habits of industry, self-control and courageous perseverence" so that they became "upright and useful members of the community". Old notions of the working-class child, as a dutiful and industrious follower of his betters, died hard.

In 1905, a *Handbook of Suggestions* for elementary teachers appeared. Teachers were now given freedom to show initiative in syllabus and method. The book was "an aid ... and a challenge to independent thought." Its thoughtful preface declared "each teacher shall think for himself, and work out such methods of teaching as may use his powers to the best advantage and be best suited to the particular needs and conditions of the school. Uniformity in details of practice ... is not desirable even if it were attainable." This was a momentous change from the old order.

Pupil-teachers gradually disappeared, candidates for teaching being encouraged to go to training college after a secondary education. Some local education authorities opened municipal colleges to meet this increased demand.

Reform of child welfare and medical care was the most important of the measures of this first decade of the century. Murmurings about poor child health in the 1890s rose to a storm during the Boer War, when half the recruits for the Army were declared unfit.

Disquieting studies of urban living conditions, like those of Charles Booth or Seebohm Rowntree, allowed Edwardian pessimists to foresee "the certainty of the approaching exhaustion of the street-bred people of Britain." (In 1904 a Government Committee on Physical Deterioration studied the matter. Its proposed remedies included medical inspection of children and provision of school meals. The Fabians wrote in support: "Without proper feeding, instruction is useless ... we put education first and food nowhere. Our children ask for bread and we give them 'a ladder'.)"

(The reforming Liberal government of 1906 introduced remedial measures. A private member's bill of 1906 (the first ever introduced by a Labour M.P.) gave L.E.A.s power to provide meals to children "unable by reason of lack of food to take full advantage of the education provided for them." A clause, placed by Morant, in a Bill of 1907 made medical inspection of children an L.E.A. duty and allowed powers of treatment.) From these six lines grew the school medical service. 1907 was later justly called "one of the great dates in our social history".

(The first school doctors' reports of 1908 were a horrifying catalogue of disease and defect. Seventy per cent of children were "dirty"; some were found sewn into their clothes. Parasites were another problem; there were cases where "the whole head appeared to be slowly moving with vermin". Defects of eyes, throat and teeth were common, as was malnutrition. The cost of the medical service was money well spent; its results were soon seen in children's faces.)

Morant's reforms ran ahead of actual practice. Edwardian memoirs convey the harshness of school life. Robert Roberts writes of Salford in *The Classic Slum* (1971), remembering the stench of classrooms with their gas lighting, the doorless privies, the "verminous notices" sent out by the Head, the consumptive teacher who had "the disgusting habit of coughing into his handkerchief, then staring at it." In a novel *Donkey Boy* (1952), Henry Williamson recalled his L.C.C. school. There was the black line on the hall floor, where offenders "toed the line" before the horrific beatings, when the Head "would haul a boy, sometimes wriggling, across the desk, and would strike him again and again with the cane, black coat-tails visibly dancing about." There was the school-friend who came barefoot: "His trousers flapped about him, having been made for a man. His jacket was too big ... he had no shirt or vest underneath, the jacket being tied across the middle with string. His white flesh was sometimes visible ..." There was the pose of the obedient pupil "sitting without movement ... his hands folded behind him to draw back his shoulders ... and his eyes looking straight ahead ..."

Most damning comments on the elementary schools were those of Edmond Holmes, Chief Inspector under Morant from 1905. In 1911, on retirement, he wrote a book, *What is and what might be*, based on a lifetime's observation. Children's imagination was neglected, he thought. Routine-ridden schools killed the child's creativity: "It will die if this kind of teaching go on ... die for lack of exercise, die wasted and atrophied by disuse." There was no independent study, key to real learning: schooling was only "blind, passive, literal, unintelligent obedience." To D. H. Lawrence, in *The Rainbow* (1916), school was part of the industrial blight of England: methods were "mechanical", teachers "machines". The school was "like a prison, with its rigid inflexible air, away from all feeling of the ordinary day".

Secondary schooling was Morant's particular interest. Some historians accuse him of distorting the natural growth of the secondary sector. Certainly he had disliked the scientific vocational bias of the Higher Grade schools and had despised the staff of the pupil-teacher centres, favouring the academic, classical tradition in which he (Winchester and Oxford), and his H.M.I. for secondary schools, J. Headlam (Eton and Cambridge), had been reared. These men shaped the new council secondary schools on a traditional grammar school pattern. The Board's *Regulations for Secondary Schools* (1904) laid down a curriculum in which literary studies balanced, even dominated, science. Latin, for instance, could not be dropped by a school without good reason.

Morant, like many of his time, favoured the idea of secondary schooling only for an élite. Places were, in any case, limited. Accordingly fees for grammar schools were fixed at £3 a year, so discouraging children of manual workers, for whom this was a fortnight's wage. The high fee was "to ensure the financial stability of the school and also to emphasize the fact that the education it provided is of a superior kind." The 1906 Liberal Government did not like such élitism. In certain districts there were already scholarships for deserving pupils. Now, under regulations of 1907, it was set down that all secondary schools receiving state grants should provide free places for a quarter of their annual entry. Thereafter the highly competitive "scholarship examination" became a crucial moment in the lives of elementary pupils. At the top of the senior school, the tangle of separate qualification examinations for various occupations was ended by the introduction of the School Certificate in 1917.

The natural growth of secondary schooling was too vigorous to be controlled entirely by Morant's regulations. From 1911 onwards, some authorities, notably London and Manchester, gathered pupils who were promising in practical studies into Central schools, offering four-year courses with a vocational bias. The L.C.C. also began Junior Technical schools in 1913. The Board watched such experiments with interest.

Morant's efforts to make secondary schooling an exclusive preserve, and his barely concealed contempt for elementary teachers, finally caused his downfall. In 1906, the N.U.T. began a feud, by calling the Board "a stronghold of class prejudice", and *The Schoolmaster* waged verbal war on Morant. The explosion came with a remark in a "strictly confidential" Board circular: "Elementary teachers are as a rule uncultured and imperfectly educated ... creatures of tradition and routine." A copy was given to a Tory M.P. and questions were asked in Parliament. A fierce press campaign forced Morant's resignation in 1911. He had made the Board into a dynamic government department, and had been the architect of the twentieth century school system.

English schooling and the First World War

The rising patriotic fervour of the pre-war years was expressed in the school world on Empire Day (May 24th), celebrated from 1906 onwards. Its aim was "to instil into the minds of children what are the privileges, the responsibilities and the duties of citizenship of the Empire." A local paper, the *Surrey Comet*, reported the day's events typically in 1914, noting that "teachers enter heartily into the spirit of the celebrations, taking care to inculcate the lessons of Empire." Even in his Salford slum school, Robert Roberts recalled teachers' quotations from Kipling or Seeley's *The Expansion of England*, and the training of the children to "Think Imperially" as they proudly contemplated red British areas on the world map. Pupils decorated themselves and their rooms in national colours, sang patriotic songs, produced tableaux, paraded the Union Jack. "A brilliant afternoon", wrote a Headmaster poignantly on the "Great Day" in the last summer of peace.

When war came, children were expected to "do their bit". They collected war materials (even horse chestnuts, supposedly used in the filters of gas masks); they dug allotments in school grounds, collected war savings through school banks (common since the Board era), visited the wounded, knitted for the troops.

Schools, like society, were drenched in propaganda. Biased textbooks explained the war to the young. In assembly, the local Roll of Honour was read, while pupils turned to salute the flag. Boys wore regimental badges, even miniatures of their fathers' uniforms. Special days were set aside to study allied countries. Pupils learned patriotic songs:

> There's a land, a dear land
> Where the rights of the free
> Are as firm as the earth
> And as wide as the sea ...
> England, wave guarded and green to the shore;
> God bless our Empire and King evermore.

Schooling suffered, as buildings were taken by the military, or turned into hospitals or refugee centres. Conscription eventually took male teachers, leaving women and volunteers to cope in schools. Double shifts were sometimes employed. The Board of Education tried to admire the expedients arranged: "The half-day out of school has sometimes been used to excellent purpose for games ... swimming, open-air work, excursions, visits to museums ..." Exceptionally, schools were actually hit by the enemy in the first air-raids. In June 1917, German Gothas bombed an infants' school in Poplar, London. Sixteen pupils died in the basement, described by a soldier witness as "choked with struggling and screaming victims, many of them crying distractedly for their mothers. Little limbs were blown from bodies, and unrecognizable remains were littered among the debris of broken desks ..."

Most damage to schooling was less spectacular. Educational retardation was optimistically estimated at three months. There were other worries for the authorities. A 1917 Report noted increase in juvenile delinquency and crime in large cities. Fathers were absent; the streets blacked out; the world sunk in violence; the temptations strong. The booming war industries also took children prematurely. Another 1917 Report commented: "Excessive hours of strenuous labour have overtaxed the powers of young people, while many have taken advantage of the extraordinary demand for juvenile labour to change from one blind alley employment to another."

Urgent action was necessary. In 1917, the Prime Minister, David Lloyd-George, introduced a scheme of national reconstruction. H. A. L. Fisher (1865–1940), Vice-Chancellor of Sheffield University, was appointed President of the Board of Education; he was to draw up educational reforms.

A major Act was passed in August 1918. It was more remarkable for the attitudes it expressed than for its actual effect. Firstly it reflected the "increased feeling of social solidarity which has been created by the war." When Fisher explained his Bill to Bristol dockers, they "rose to their feet two or three times in the course of my speech, waved their handkerchiefs and cheered themselves hoarse. The prospect of wider opportunities ... open to the disinherited filled them with enthusiasm."

Secondly, the Act ended the notion of elementary schooling as a kind of charity, or simply as preparation for work. The sacrifices of the war had shown, claimed Fisher, "that the boundaries of citizenship are not determined by wealth" and "that the industrial workers of the country are entitled to be considered primarily as citizens and as fit subjects for any form of education." Ordinary families valued education not merely to help them earn more but "because they know that in the treasures of the mind they can find ... a refuge from the necessary hardships of a life spent in the midst of clanging machinery."

The Act aimed "to repair the war's intellectual wastage" and to limit "industrial pressure on the child life of this country". School life was to be extended, beginning earlier in projected L.E.A. nursery schools and ending, without exception, at fourteen. The "half-timers" (there were still 70,000 counted in 1911) disappeared. Employment of school-age children, except on part-time delivery rounds, was forbidden. The familiar newspaper boys, even the pantomime "imps", were no more. Projected "continuation schools" were to teach young people part-time up to eighteen.

Another theme of the Act was that "children ... shall not be debarred from receiving the benefits of any form of education by which they are capable of profiting through inability to pay fees." Elementary schools were now to be completely free, and new "percentage grants" would help finance secondary schooling. The medical service was extended to older pupils and L.E.A.s encouraged to provide playing fields, swimming baths and school camps.

In these ways, the state would "secure for its juvenile population conditions under which mind, body and character may be harmoniously developed." Although many of the Act's proposals soon foundered in the economic crisis, its spirit set the tone for the work of post-war reformers.

English schooling 1919–39

The fine hopes of the Fisher Act were soon dimmed. The depression of 1921 caused the government to form a committee (chaired by Sir Eric Geddes) to consider cuts in public spending. The so-called "Geddes Axe" (1922) reduced education expenditure by a third. The "day continuation" schools were slaughtered: nursery schooling was not only stopped, it was even suggested that the age of school entry should rise to six. Fisher had worked to improve teachers' salaries and pensions by instituting the Burnham Committee to standardize payment. Now these salaries were cut. Teacher–pupil ratios increased. In 1922, a quarter of elementary classes still had more than sixty pupils.

There was reaction against such ill-advised economies when Britain's first Labour Government took office in 1924, in the mildly revolutionary atmosphere of the mid 'twenties. The Labour movement had long valued education as a magic touchstone which would bring a better life to working-class families. Many of the new men of influence had had only the rudiments of learning. Ernest Bevin, of the Transport and General Workers' Union, had left school at eleven to be a farm boy; J. H. Thomas, of the Railwaymen, had been an errand boy at eight; Ben Turner, of the Textile Workers, had been a "half-timer" in a cotton mill. Labour members felt their lack of learning to be a handicap in Commons debate. They were therefore ready to support increased opportunity in education.

The 1918 Labour programme had proposed a school system "which shall get rid of all class distinctions and privileges", bringing to each child "the training—physical, mental and moral—of which he is capable." The Labour slogan of the 'twenties was "secondary education for all". A policy book with that title appeared in 1922, edited by R. H. Tawney, the socialist writer and philosopher. He sought to end that "organization on lines of class which is the tragedy of English education". Universal secondary schooling to sixteen should be the Labour aim.

Secondary education in 1924 was only for a minority. On one hand there were the great public schools, whose fees deterred all but the rich (Eton, for instance, charged £210 a year, more than the annual income of a skilled worker). On the other were grammar schools, charging fees (of some £13 per annum) to all but the twenty-five per cent who were scholarship winners. Two-thirds of their pupils were lower-middle-class: the grammar school, according to a sardonic politician, was "a social factory for turning the sons of clerks and shopkeepers into clerks and shopkeepers." Only one child in ten went to grammar school, but the war had sharpened social ambition. By 1920 11,000 pupils were refused free places, despite passing the examination, and other children, who were accepted, could not afford fares and uniforms. The "scholarship ladder", said Tawney, was better described as a "greasy pole".

In 1924, Charles Trevelyan, Commons spokesman on education, announced that the number of grammar school free places was to be doubled. Even the Conservatives, seeing the need for more "white collar" workers, approved, though the right-wing Federation of British Industry declared that "care should be taken to avoid creating ... a large class of persons whose education is unsuitable for the employment they eventually follow."

Trevelyan also asked the Consultative Committee of the Board of Education (chaired by Sir W. H. Hadow) to report on secondary education outside the grammar schools. The Hadow Report, *The Education of the Adolescent*, was published in 1926. It concluded that only five per cent of children over eleven were doing post-elementary work in "Senior Departments", or in Central or Junior Technical Schools. Too many of these courses were "like the rope which the Indian juggler throws into the air to end in vacancy". The Report therefore suggested a complete reorganization of schooling, now conceived as a single continuous process in two stages: "primary" up to eleven, and "secondary" up to fifteen, the proposed minimum leaving age. Alongside grammar schools, "modern schools" were to be developed for the average child, where "practical and realistic studies" were to be tempered by "a general and humane education". Such schools would have three aims: "the forming and strengthening of character"; "the training of boys and girls to delight in pursuits and rejoice in accomplishments" and "the awakening ... of the practical intelligence for ... service of the community." Children with real practical skills were to transfer to Junior Technical schools at thirteen.

These proposals were officially approved, but delayed in practice. The massive economic depression in the early 1930s crippled educational progress. The free place system was abolished in 1931, and the means-tested "special place" substituted. The raising of the leaving age was postponed, and the large building grant to support Hadow schemes was withdrawn. By 1938, only sixty-five per cent of senior pupils attended reorganized schools, although seventy-two per cent now had some secondary schooling. Confused, inadequate education was still the experience of many and the "all-in" elementary school was a long time dying, especially in rural areas.

The inter-war period was a time when experiments and novel teaching methods coloured even official reports. Efforts were made to make lessons more interesting. Instead of learning conceived as a "grind" or "stiffening process" (noted a 1921 Report on English Teaching) there should be "a living interest and a sense of purpose" in class work. The 1926 Hadow Report boldly suggested that the barriers between school and community should be dissolved and "the real world" brought to the classroom.

A second Hadow Report on the primary school (1931) was more radical in tone. School was to teach children how to live. Learning was best based on "the experience, the curiosity and interests of children themselves." This eloquent Report became the basis of modern primary practice: "What a wise and good parent would desire for his own children, that a nation must desire for all its children." It was heavily coloured by the ideas of Maria Montessori, an Italian pioneer whose work with infants in Rome had been described in *The Montessori Method* (1912). "Useful spontaneous activity" in the child, using the carefully-designed Montessori apparatus under the teacher's guidance, was contrasted with the sterility of the conventional school where "children, like butterflies mounted on pins, are fastened each to his place, the desk, spreading the useless wings of barren and meaningless knowledge ... immobile and silent."

Novel teaching devices appeared in schools. The British Film Institute (founded 1933) sponsored educational films, which could be hired (with projector) for school use. Radio lessons to schools were even more dramatic. John Reith (later, Lord Reith), the first Director-General of the British Broadcasting Corporation (founded 1922), was convinced of the immense educational value of the wireless medium, which should "carry into the greatest possible number of homes everything that is best in every department of human knowledge, endeavour and achievement." In particular, schools broadcasts, started in 1924, were to bring children "into direct contact with the greatest authorities of the century". In 1927, controlled experiment was carried on in Kent schools to refine techniques. French and music were obvious successes, but best remembered of schools programmes were episodes of dramatized history: "Boys and girls of other days", and "How things began". Programme pamphlets were mostly sold to elementary schools, but some grammar schools joined in "Unfinished Debates" in the 1930s allowing them to discuss such topics as "Talkies are no improvement on the silent film" or "Disarmament is impracticable at the present time".

Educational psychology became influential at this time. Intelligence tests, devised in Europe before the Great War, were adapted for English use by Cyril Burt, L.C.C. psychologist after 1922. Their use in scholarship examinations became widespread for many years. The nature of child development and learning was increasingly discussed. The revelations of Freud about the formation of personality also affected the treatment of delinquent children. The American, Homer Lane, had experimented at his New Common-wealth school in Hampshire during the war by withdrawing authority and allowing pupils wide freedom. A. S. Neill's Summerhill, in Suffolk, was a similar, more enduring "free school", where children chose their lessons and practised self-government.

Best documented of such advanced schools was the Malting House in Cambridge, founded in 1924 by a wealthy businessman, Geoffrey Pyke, who invited a psychologist, Susan Isaacs, to teach a small group of young children. She was to allow pupils "the fullest opportunities for healthy growth in every direction" and to "observe what children do under free conditions, and study the laws of growth". In the large house and garden, pupils were free to try many activities, while their talk and work were meticulously recorded by Mrs. Isaacs. Rumour soon spread unjust stories of bad language and behaviour, of frequent bonfires, of the dissection of the school cat, yet the school won an extraordinary reputation, especially when a film was made of its work. Its brief career ended in 1927, and Susan Isaacs departed to write classic textbooks on child development.

Although official control of design was strict and funds limited, the inter-war period produced pleasant school buildings. One-storey, pavilion-style schools were a fashion. Concern with ventilation and a fashion for "open-air" schooling allowed whole walls to be opened by folding back glazed doors.

Remarkable buildings were created in the Cambridgeshire Village College experiment. Henry Morris (1889–1961) was Chief Education Officer of the County after 1922. His *Memorandum on the Village College* (1924) was an ambitious plan not only to solve the long-standing problem of rural schooling, but to provide educational and social centres that would revive whole communities. The College would house a day school for children, evening classes for adults, and provide space for community activities: library, welfare centre, British Legion and so on. This "many-sided institution ... would be a visible demonstration in stone of the continuity and never-ceasingness of education."

The first Village College, at Sawston, near Cambridge, was opened in 1930. By diligent fund-raising, Morris opened three more before the Second World War. The buildings were to rival the churches as focal points in the English rural landscape, expressing its spirit, "something of its humaneness and modesty, something of the age-long and permanent dignity of husbandry." Impington was Morris's masterpiece, designed by the famous German architect, Walter Gropius, and the Englishman, Maxwell Fry. The result was described as "one of the best buildings of its date in England ... a pattern for much to come." Beautiful grounds set off the elegant building, following Morris's belief that a fine environment could develop the taste and spirit of College pupils. The art critic, Herbert Read, called Impington "a practical demonstration of idealism in education."

The opening of Impington in September, 1939, coincided with the outbreak of war: the first event of its life was the digging of slit trenches on the field as shelter against air-raids. The College was to feature in wartime propaganda, on film and poster, and was to be mentioned in debates about the Butler Act, as an epitome of the best of English educational achievement that the nation was fighting to preserve.

The Second World War: disruption and reform

The coming of war in 1939 caused a huge social upheaval in England. Fear of air bombing led to mass evacuation of the population from threatened areas. Plans had been given to Local Authorities in 1938: the country was divided into evacuation, neutral and reception areas. Schoolchildren, one of the priority classes, would move from the first (mainly urban industrial districts) to the last (mainly in the countryside), with their teachers. In spring 1939, meetings were held to explain details to parents, though participation was voluntary.

"Operation Pied Piper" began on September 1, 1939. Clutching gas masks, shepherded by teachers, who had devised banners and labels for their flocks, children packed all available trains and were swept off to vaguely-known destinations. One and a half million people were moved in three days, in a "triumph of preparation, organization and discipline". Reception was less efficient: schools were scattered over wide areas and billeting methods were often less than satisfactory.

For city children, rural England could be a shock: some were surprised to find that apples grew on trees, that cows (seen only in books) were bigger than dogs. Hosts were also shocked. "Complaints are pouring in about the half-savage, verminous and wholly illiterate children from slums who have been billeted on clean homes", noted a *Times* correspondent. "Stories are told of mattresses and carpets polluted, of wilful despoliation and dirt that one would associate only with untrained animals." There were scabies and headlice, children sewn into clothes, or shod with cardboard. Public opinion was impressed by this revelation of the condition of poor children. H. G. Wells in *The New World Order*, (1940) relished the idea that "parasites have been spread, as if in a passion of equalitarian propaganda ... throughout the length and breadth of the land."

In the reception areas, children attended school on a shift system, or roamed the beaches and lanes with teachers, studying natural history or geography. Children often flourished: a letter in the *Times Educational Supplement* described how "some children from a poor area have become almost unrecognizable within a few weeks. One small girl was so chubby that she needed a new gas-mask."

Secondary school evacuation could not be so haphazard. Schools were twinned, where possible, to allow continuity of study.

Independent schools took in pupils from a dangerous district. Thus Lancing accommodated Westminster, and Wellington took St. Paul's. Eton gallantly stayed in Windsor, boys attending school bare-headed to avoid fights over top-hats on the way to shelters. Some children of wealthy parents were sent to America or parts of the Empire to escape the war entirely.

Children remaining in cities or drifting home from evacuation became a severe problem, as schools were closed or requisitioned by the military, or Civil Defence. Streets were "loud with children". According to a *Times* correspondent: "There are parts of great industrial towns where any strolling observer will find streets full of children revelling in freedom which they were not meant to enjoy." They were "running wild", some taking jobs, others drifting into crime. Home-tuition schemes were inadequate. In late 1939, parliamentary protest forced the government to re-open schools provided with adequate shelters, though evacuees were discouraged from returning. In the confusion, thousands went untaught.

Further waves of evacuation in 1940 complicated confusion, as fear of invasion removed children from south and east-coast towns, and the actuality of the Blitz stimulated movement from cities. "Trickle evacuation" continued throughout the war, the public being moved to action by the horror of certain incidents. Thus, in 1943, a hit-and-run raid by a single plane struck Sandhurst Road School, Lewisham, killing six teachers and seven children and injuring fifty others. Although by 1944 some normality of schooling had been recovered, it was lost again as Flying Bombs and V-2 rockets fell on London, causing another mass evacuation.

The effects of war on children could not be entirely calculated: air-raid disruptions, changes of staff, the restless family movement hindered intellectual progress. Average retardation of a year was reported from tests on war pupils. The substantial proportion of illiterate youths among post-war National Servicemen revealed these hidden scars of war.

Physically, children benefited from the expansion of medical services in wartime. Fear of epidemics following bombing led to diphtheria vaccination of nearly seven million children, which soon reduced deaths. The modest school meals and milk services of pre-war times were massively expanded. By 1945, L.E.A.s were supplying two million dinners a day; milk, too, reached nearly eighty per cent of schoolchildren.

Social reform became a secondary aim of the war, symbolized in the huge queues to buy the Beveridge Report (1942), the blueprint for post-war social security. It was "a time for revolutions, not for patching" noted Sir William Beveridge. In this spirit, the Board of Education planned a reformed education service.

The Board had declined in status since Morant's time, its President's post having become a political backwater. The ill-fated Act of 1936 with its abortive plan to raise the leaving age to fifteen in 1939, had typified a decade of sluggish growth and financial shortage, overlooked by ineffectual Presidents. In wartime, the Board's handling of post-evacuation confusion brought fierce public criticism. Its civil servants, evacuated to Bournemouth, answered attacks by preparing, in 1941, "*Education after the War*", a bold plan, better known as "The Green Book", which was circulated to interested parties for their comments. At the same time, education found a fresh champion in R. A. Butler (b. 1902), Board President from 1941.

By July 1943, after wide-ranging discussions which included such topics as the dual system, the public schools, the leaving age and equality of opportunity, Butler had prepared a White Paper, "*Educational Reconstruction*". It proposed "to recast the national education service", because "in the youth of the nation we have our greatest national asset." In a Commons debate on the plan, the House (according to a *Times* reporter) "showed itself of one mind, to a degree rare in parliamentary annals ... not a single voice was raised in favour of holding up ... any of the proposals for educational advance."

Butler, and his Parliamentary Secretary, J. Chuter-Ede, introduced a Bill in December 1943. By August 4, 1944, it became law, after amiable debate, influenced no doubt by the improved war news.

The President now became Minister of Education, given more power to direct and control development. L.E.A.s were reformed to minimize their differences: the smaller Part III Authorities were abolished, reducing the number of authorities from 315 to 146.

Education was now defined as "a continuous process, arranged in three stages: primary, secondary and further". Each L.E.A. was to survey local need and submit reorganization plans to the Ministry. Schools were to be "sufficient in number, character and equipment to afford for all pupils opportunities for education ... as may be described in view of their different ages, abilities and aptitudes."

There were plans (not to be fulfilled) for nursery schools, and for County Colleges, which would give part-time schooling for those who left before eighteen. The secondary leaving age was to be raised to fifteen (this happened in 1947) and eventually to sixteen, when it was possible (this was delayed until 1973). All fees for maintained schools were abolished, as every child was to receive secondary schooling. Privately-owned schools (about 10,000 in number) were to be registered and inspected.

Parental duty was defined: they were to cause their child to receive "efficient full-time education suitable to his age, aptitude and ability." There were parental rights, too: "as far as is practicable, pupils are to be educated in accordance with the wishes of their parents."

Butler boldly tackled the problem of the dual system. The first Hadow report had vividly described the lingering religious problem as "difficult ground (where) there are fires burning beneath the thin crust on which we tread". It remained a major preoccupation of the 1944 debates. By Butler's compromise, church schools could now be "controlled" (whereby the L.E.A. took complete financial responsibility) or "aided" (whereby they continued independent, with the L.E.A. paying half the cost of maintenance). Half the Church of England schools soon became controlled, while the 2,000 Catholic schools firmly opted for aided status. There was to be, for the first time, compulsory religious education in every school, the only part of the curriculum actually set down by law. Furthermore "the school day ... shall begin with collective worship on the part of all pupils": thus the frequently joyless religious assembly became familiar in the school experience. These measures concluded the centuries-old religious difficulty. The socialist Aneurin Bevan protested that "the Church of England gets the biggest bite out of this Bill everywhere" and condemned the Church's "secret, furtive influence". Yet, in reality, the school world, like society about it, was to be increasingly secular in post-war years.

The broad scale of the Butler Act made it the most impressive educational measure in English history, and it remains the foundation of the contemporary school system. A Ministry survey of public opinion in 1945 noted that many people had been dissatisfied with their own schooling and were pleased for "everybody to have an equal chance" in the improved order.

Post-war problems

When peace came in 1945, there were immense problems about putting the Butler Act into effect. Enemy action had destroyed or damaged thousands of schools (1,150 of 1,200 London schools had suffered). Private housing had first claim on labour and building materials, yet the post-war Labour government made determined efforts. Ellen Wilkinson, the Education Minister, arranged for a supply of prefabricated classrooms under the H.O.R.S.A. scheme (Hutting Operation for the Raising of the School Age). The 1945 Building regulations set ambitious standards: kitchens, specialist rooms, playing fields were now essentials. By contrast a 1948 survey described inadequate buildings left from the past: "two-storey red-brick buildings, whose architects, uncertain as to whether their model schemes should be a church, a barracks, or a railway-station, created something solid, serviceable and ugly." Rooms were "horribly dark. Gas is still the means of artificial light ... there are dark dungeon-like passages." Gradually, in the 1950s, bright new buildings began to rise, especially on housing estates.

A shortage of teachers had already been foreseen in wartime, and an emergency training scheme was launched in 1943, which produced about 35,000 teachers by 1951. Long-term improvements in the situation had been studied by the McNair Report (1944) which suggested a three-year course, better salaries, a relaxation on the ban on married women teachers and withdrawal of the "pledge" to teach, that was a condition of many students' grants. Even these efforts could not easily reduce class sizes. The birth-rate, in decline before the war, suddenly increased by some 700,000 in the post-war "Bulge". Well into the 1960s, there were classes of over forty, or even fifty in some primary schools.

The public schools had been much discussed during the war. These schools had continued to be popular between the wars, although a vogue for autobiographical novels, following Alec Waugh's *Loom of Youth* (1917) had mocked their ideals and methods. Though there had been new foundations, such as Stowe (1923) and Bryanston (1928), there were also financial problems which caused some schools to adopt Direct Grant status, (State financial aid sent direct from the Board, by-passing the Local Authority). In the 1930s pupil numbers had fallen, and some smaller schools had closed. The war had doubled these problems: costs soared and evacuated schools looked unattractive to the parent.

In 1942, the Fleming Committee was appointed to consider how public schools could be linked to the state system, thus qualifying them for government aid. The democratic mood of the time led to over-optimistic newspaper headlines: "Public schools for all plan"; "Every bright boy and girl will go to public school."

Opinions expressed to the Committee were predictable. R. H. Tawney, speaking for the Left, doubted whether "the existence of a group of schools reserved for the children of the comparatively prosperous ... is in the best interests of the nation." For the Conservatives, the schools were "too valuable to be jeopardized", making "a special contribution". The Fleming Report (1944) suggested schemes to open the public schools to all children "capable of profiting thereby, irrespective of the income of their parents". Under Scheme A of the Fleming Report, L.E.A.s could reserve places at direct grant schools; under Scheme B, the larger public schools would reserve a quarter of their places for pupils who had attended state primaries. Both proposals were quietly set aside. The L.E.A.s disliked the extra cost; state Heads resented poaching of their best pupils; the mechanics of selection seemed formidable. After 1945, the public schools entered a period of fresh prosperity that allowed them to forget the need for state aid. Many a liberal parent, seeking the best schooling for his child, has found himself in the dilemma described in a letter of 1948 by the left-wing writer, George Orwell: "Obviously it is democratic for everyone to go to the same schools ... but when you see what the elementary schools are like ... you feel that any child that has the chance should be rescued from them. I remember in 1936 meeting John Strachey ... then a Communist Party member ... and him telling me he had just had a son and was putting him down for Eton ... he said that, given our existing society, it was the best education ... in principle, I don't feel sure that he was wrong."

A major preoccupation of educational discussion since 1945 has been the organization of state secondary schooling. The 1944 Act did not specify any particular arrangement but guidance to L.E.A.s had been given by two official reports, Spens (1938) and Norwood (1943). Both supported the original Hadow scheme for a "tripartite" structure of grammar, technical and modern schools. Spens declared that "a simple liberal or general education for all is impracticable (and) varying forms of education were to be evolved in order to meet the needs of boys and girls, differing widely in intellectual and emotional capacity." It boldly declared that intelligence tests could distinguish these various types of child. Norwood further defined the three categories: the grammar school child "who is interested in learning for its own sake"; the technical pupil "who often has an uncanny insight into the intricacies of mechanism", and the modern pupil "who deals more easily with concrete things than with ideas ... (and who) is interested only in the moment (and is) essentially practical." Such fallacious divisions won wide support because they easily fitted the existing system. "The suggestion of the Committee seems to be that the Almighty has benevolently created three types of child in just those proportions which would justify educational administrators," commented the historian S. J. Curtis, with sarcasm, in *History of Education in Great Britain* (1967).

An alternative to the tripartite system was the "multilateral school" discussed by Spens. All secondary-age pupils would attend a single school, where they would be divided into appropriate streams. Variants were the bilateral school with "grammar" and "modern" sides, or the "school base", where various types of school would be grouped around a common central block housing special facilities (concert hall, craft rooms, chapel, canteen) with a large tract of open land nearby for recreation.

The Labour government of 1945 supported tripartism. In the pamphlet *The New Secondary Education* (1947), the Ministry noted that "different types (of school) will be needed to meet the differences that exist between children". Given their existing facilities and financial problems most L.E.A.s were content to submit plans on these lines. Yet five intended to try multilateral or "comprehensive" schools, and twenty-five others were to carry out "experiments".

Most ambitious was London's "School Plan" of 1947, which decided on partial comprehensive reorganization, after tests with eight large secondary school pioneers. Its first purpose-built comprehensive was opened at Kidbrooke in 1954, attracting thousands of visitors to its splendid buildings and creating controversy in Parliament and press as local grammar schools closed. Whereas comprehensive schemes were accepted in rural areas (Anglesey, for example, was non-selective by 1958), there was resentment in suburban districts. The Headmaster of Watford Grammar School expressed this opposition in 1956, fearing "death by drowning in the deep waters of the comprehensive school." He looked uneasily at the L.C.C. "which marches blindly forward under the comprehensive school banner undeterred by criticism from the profession or by the anguish of parents." The fierce battle over the proposed scheme for Middlesex, abandoned in 1949 when Labour lost control of the Council, was a portent of many disputes, fought with all the bitterness that had earlier characterized religious divisions in the school world. The war of words began: comprehensives were "enormous and unwieldy", "factory schools" or "unproven experiments".

In the 1950s the best grammar schools flourished, under the stimulus of the reformed public examinations: the General Certificate of Education (G.C.E.), at Ordinary and Advanced level, begun in 1951. They produced a "meritocracy" from an ambitious clientele (the number of Sixth Form students increased by half between 1953 and 1960). A minority attended technical schools which were never widely established. The majority went to secondary modern schools (there were three of these to each grammar school). Despite devoted teaching and individual successes, they were without tradition, inheriting only the mantle of the elementary school, and never achieved the "parity of esteem" looked for by the Norwood Report. The delay in raising the leaving age to sixteen cut off many children's education prematurely. The Crowther Report of 1959 (on pupils aged 16 to 18) stated that "the education that is provided for the great mass of children is inadequate both in its quality and its duration." The Newsom Report of 1963 (on the average secondary pupil) stressed the waste of talent in secondary modern education: "There is little doubt that among our children there are reserves of ability which can be tapped." These "unexpected reserves of talent" should be used "in the national economic interest".

Public opinion came to think of eleven-plus selection as "the scholarship", which a child passed or failed. On average, one child in five attended a grammar school, but, in practice, places were unevenly provided. In the 1950s disquiet about the fairness of the "eleven-plus" grew. Intelligence testing, a crucial part of the selection process, was falling into disrepute. "Late-developers" — children who matured intellectually later in adolescence— were a serious problem. Sociologists, increasingly influential commentators on the nation's schooling, showed how poor social background distorted test results for working-class children. Thus *Social Class and Educational Opportunity* (1956) by J. Floud and A. Halsey claimed that the eleven-plus examination was too often a social divider rather than a fair assessment of intellectual ability.

As the standard of living rose during the 1950s and '60s, educational opportunity, an important part of the average family's ambitions, became a public preoccupation second only in importance to the cost of living, and so grew into a major domestic political issue.

During their long period of opposition from 1951 to 1964, the Labour Party moved from mild belief in tripartism to whole-hearted support of the comprehensive principle. In 1959, the Labour manifesto *Signposts for the Sixties* advocated equality of opportunity in schooling as a major theme. By 1963, cleverly sensing public opinion, Harold Wilson, the Labour leader, was supporting a comprehensive school policy in his broad plan for national revival. After their victory of 1964, Labour moved boldly into total reform of the state secondary sector, despite inadequate evidence about the merits of comprehensive schools. This was in the teeth of Conservative opposition which, after years of uncertainty, now firmly supported the grammar schools. Robert Cooke, Conservative M.P. for Bristol, expressed typical sentiments about "some sinister national plan of the Labour party to destroy fine schools which are now doing a splendid job of work, and to impose unwanted on the country a pattern which is only just beginning to be effective."

In July 1965, the Department of Education and Science (as the Ministry became in 1964) issued *Circular 10/65*. Its architect was the Secretary of State, Anthony Crosland (1928–1977). L.E.A.s were requested to submit plans for comprehensive reorganization within twelve months. Various recommended schemes would be considered suitable: an 11–18 all-through school; the three-tier system, with a middle school from 8 to 12; or various forms of two-tier schools with divisions at 14 or 16. Most L.E.A.s, further stimulated by the threat of a Bill to compel them to act, co-operated in this major revolution. Fierce argument has continued ever since, but the tendency created by the circular is not to be denied.

I count upon the support of our countrymen to enable us to close for ever those barren controversies which for too long have oocupied our time, and, in the interests alike of parental liberty and of educational efficiency, to terminate the present system of costly confusion.

A. J. BALFOUR
Introducing the 1902 Education Bill

The purpose of the public elementary school is to form and strengthen the character and to develop the intelligence of the children entrusted to it, and to make the best use of the school years available, in assisting both boys and girls … to fit themselves, practically as well as intellectually, for the work of life.

Board of Education: 1904 Code of Regulations.

The stunted child elongates slightly in time, but remains very thin, loses colour, the muscles remain small. The legs are inclined to become bowed …

    The girls exhibit the same shortness of stature, the same miserable development … The same sallow cheeks and carious teeth.

Report on poor children
Committee on Physical Deterioration (1904)

What is the meaning of Empire Day?
Why do the cannons roar?
Why does the cry "God save the King"
Echo from shore to shore?
Every year we homage pay
To our banner proud
That has never bowed.
And that's the meaning of Empire Day!

School song for Empire Day (1914)

We fight for honour. You know what honour is among schoolboys—straight dealing, truth speaking, and 'playing the game'. Well, we are standing up for honour among nations, while Germany is playing the sneak and bully in the big European school. Germany must be taught to 'play cricket', to play fair, to honour 'a scrap of paper' …

SIR JAMES YOXALL
Pamphlet for schools: *Why Britain went to War* (1916)

(We have) overdrawn our account with posterity … I conceive that it is part of the duty of our generation to provide some means for compensating the tragic loss which our nation is enduring … by the creation of a system of education … which will increase the value of every human unit in the whole of society.

H. A. L. FISHER
Commons speech (1917)

A real guarantee will have been given to the working classes that their sons and daughters will find the doors of life opening to their knock. Such a guarantee gives them the fair share of freedom and justice which we tell them we are fighting to maintain: it gives a concrete value and meaning to an abstract ideal.

Comment on the 1918 Education Act.
The Times, August 9th, 1918.

The organization of education on lines of class ... has been at once a symptom, an effect and a cause of the control of the lives of the mass of men and women by a privileged minority. The very assumption on which it is based, that all the child of the worker needs is "elementary education"—as though the mass of the people, like anthropoid apes, had fewer convolutions in their brains than the rich—is in itself a piece of insolence.

R. H. TAWNEY
Secondary Education for All (1922)

There is a tide which begins to rise in the veins of youth at the age of eleven or twelve. It is called by the name of adolescence. If that tide can be taken at the flood, and a new voyage begun ... we think that it will "move on to fortune" ...

The Hadow Report, 1926.

The curriculum of the primary school is to be thought of in terms of activity and experience, rather than of knowledge to be acquired and facts to be stored ...

The Hadow Report, 1931.

The first time I heard a broadcast was by accident in a country school-house where ... the school mistress had installed a wireless set ... She and I and the three most musical of her pupils ... listened to a talk on music by Sir Walford Davies ... The children's eyes were round with wonder. We grown-ups were exalted. Beauty could now enter every home and every classroom.

MARY SOMERVILLE
First Head of Schools Broadcasting

I watched the children having the time of their lives, wading up to their knees, trying to fill a sandpit with water, mending a tap with a spanner, oiling the works of a clock, joyously feeding a bonfire, dissecting crabs, climbing on scaffolding, weighing each other on a see-saw, weaving, modelling, working lathes—in fact, doing all those things which every child delights in doing. At Malting House School, children's dreams come true ...

Review of the film of Malting House School
The Spectator (July, 1927)

Except for a small number the children were filthy, and in this district we have never seen so many verminous children lacking any knowledge of clean and hygienic habits. Furthermore, it appeared they were unbathed for months ... others had septic sores all over their bodies ... the appalling apathy of the mothers was terrible to see.
Women's Institute Report on Evacuees (1940)

The future of the world is to the highly educated races, who alone can handle the scientific apparatus necessary for pre-eminence in peace or survival in war.
WINSTON CHURCHILL
Broadcast (1943)

The Government's purpose is to secure for children a happier childhood and a better start in life ... It is the object of the present proposals to strengthen and inspire the younger generation for it is as true today, as when it was first said, that "the bulwarks of a city are its men".
White Paper, *Educational Reconstruction* (1943)

A Bill which is at one and the same time a masterpiece of compromise and an inspiring embodiment of educational advance.
Comment on the Bill that became the 1944 Education Act
The Times (December 17th, 1943)

The trend of social development is leaving the public schools out of alignment with the world in which they exist ... (we see) the unreality of an educational system which segregates so thoroughly the boys of one class from those of another in a world where ... they will meet in later life as equals.
The Fleming Report on the Public Schools (1944)

Mr. and Mrs. Brown, the ordinary parents of this country, do not feel aggrieved because their Tommy goes to a council school, while little Lord Pantalduke goes to Eton; but what does grieve them is that Jimmy Jones over the road has a scholarship to the grammar school while their Tommy has to stay in the modern school.
ALICE BACON M.P.
Labour Party Conference (1953)

As Socialists, and Democrats, we oppose this system of educational apartheid, because we believe in equality of opportunity. But that is not all. We simply cannot as a nation afford to neglect the educational development of a single boy or girl. We cannot afford to cut off three-quarters or more of our children from virtually any chance of higher education.
HAROLD WILSON, Labour leader
Labour Party Conference (1963)

It is the Government's declared objective to end selection at eleven plus and to eliminate separation in secondary education ... The Secretary of State accordingly requests local education authorities ... to prepare and submit to him plans for reorganizing secondary education in their areas on comprehensive lines ...

ANTHONY CROSLAND
Circular 10/65 (1965)

Epilogue: into the nineteen-seventies

The 1967 Plowden Report, which surveyed progress in primary school education since the war, was an expression of the progressivism of the late 1960s. The most important advance had been a reduction in the size of classes. Only three per cent of the primary school population of four million children remained in teaching groups containing more than forty pupils. The Report mentioned other improvements: the best of the new school buildings—some with an open-plan structure reflecting novel approaches to class activity—that attracted world-wide interest; the experiments in junior mathematics teaching; the use of "creative writing" in English written work; the adoption in some schools of the Initial Teaching Alphabet (I.T.A.) as an aid to reading; the adoption of discovery methods in elementary science studies. The Report was coloured by the work of psychologists, especially Jean Piaget who identified certain stages of child development. Accordingly, it suggested twelve or thirteen, rather than eleven, as a better age for transfer to secondary school (thus encouraging several L.E.A.s to develop "middle schools").

Yet the sociologist had become the most important educational theorist of the 1960s. The Report noted how closely associated were social circumstances and academic achievement. Concern was therefore expressed about "education priority areas" (E.P.A.s) which "for generations have been starved of new schools, new houses and new investment". More educational resources and effort were to be devoted to these areas. Among the E.P.A.s were districts of immigrant settlement. In primary schools there were over 100,000 immigrant children, many with special problems arising from a limited knowledge of English. By 1970, after extensive efforts, pupils with such problems made up a mere sixteen per cent of the total immigrant school population.

Nursery education remained a major area for improvement. Progress had been slow since the 1918 Act had first given Authorities permission to give such schooling. By the 1960s, some areas provided generously; some did nothing. Two factors stimulated action: a growing appreciation, learned from psychologists, of the vital importance of the infant years on a child's intellectual development, and the ever-growing tendency for married women to go out to work. Grants for nursery education were improved in 1968, especially to E.P.A.s. A Conservative White Paper of 1972 proposed systematic provision of pre-school education but progress has been hindered by financial stringency.

State secondary education since 1965 has been dominated by questions of organization and curriculum. The demand for longer secondary schooling continued to increase as a factor in the rising standard of living. By 1970, fifteen per cent of seventeen-year-olds were still at school as compared with twelve per cent in 1962. The minimum school leaving age was finally raised to sixteen in 1972, thus fulfilling the long-cherished dream of providing adequate secondary education for all.

Comprehensive reorganization, following a variety of schemes (some with middle schools, or with Sixth Form Colleges), continued steadily after 1968. One hundred and fifteen L.E.A.s had submitted their plans by 1970 and only ten had refused to present any scheme. Opposition has hardened, however, in the 'Seventies. As the first conviction of the comprehensive school pioneers has faded, so conservative opposition has fought to preserve the remaining grammar schools, loth to have their record of academic excellence abandoned and seeing the comprehensive school as a threat to parental choice. Yet the issue, however hotly debated in the popular press, is already dead. The country's educational resources are already committed to the comprehensive system. For the rest of the century, debate will centre on the curriculum of the secondary school.

The 1960s also saw the beginning of a revolution in the work of the schools. Academic targets are provided by two examinations taken by sixteen-year-olds. The General Certificate of Education (G.C.E.), first set in 1951, is intended for the ablest pupils. It is controlled by examining Boards, which have links with the universities. The Certificate of Secondary Education (C.S.E.), which began in 1965, is intended for pupils of average ability. Teachers, who administer local Boards, have more control over the syllabus and management. The Schools Council (set up by the Ministry of Education in 1964 to "secure a happier marriage between the actual work of the schools ... and the examinations") was, by 1971, already proposing a new 16+ examination to be taken by all secondary school pupils as a logical step from the comprehensive idea.

There was much experiment in curriculum and teaching methods in the 1960s: the Nuffield science teaching project (begun in 1962) led the way, preparing improved teaching materials drawn up after extensive consultation with teachers. These often used the "discovery" principle. Technical aids—the language laboratory, closed-circuit television, even computer terminals—became more common in schools at this time.

The 'Seventies have also seen progress in the professional training and status of the teacher. In 1969 it was decided that, by 1974, all teachers in maintained schools should have passed a course of professional training. The James Report on "Teacher Education and Training" (1972) proposed an all-graduate profession, with three-year B.Ed. degrees as a minimum qualification. In-service training was strengthened by widespread establishment of Teachers' Centres, where new developments in subject teaching could be discussed. In the secondary sector, there has also been a quiet revolution in management techniques in both the pastoral and academic structures of schools.

The ambitions of the 1944 Fleming Report on the public schools have remained unfulfilled. Labour governments have been concerned with the social privilege conferred by a public school education, though the great cost of a possible state take-over has prohibited direct action. A Public Schools Commission reported on the independent sector of education in 1968. Although the commissioners noted improvements made in the schools since the war, most notably in their record of academic success, they also thought they were a socially divisive influence. A scheme was proposed to make half the places at public school available to state-maintained pupils, especially those coming from deprived backgrounds with a "boarding need". Independent day and direct grant schools should become part of the state system. Nothing was done to implement these proposals. Despite rising costs and the need to charge higher and higher fees, the public schools still remain proudly independent, the best of them attracting a world-wide clientele and winning unrivalled academic distinctions. Only direct grant schools have become an actual political issue, with successive Labour governments reducing and then abolishing their state subsidies (forcing some schools into complete independence) while the Conservatives remain pledged to their support.

Education has always been a mirror of its age. After the expansion and vitality of the 1960s, the economic depression of the 1970s has brought a loss of confidence in educational purpose and progress. Both political and public opinion has grown querulous, whatever the evidence of statistics about actual improvements. Faces are set to an imagined better time in the past when standards were higher and discipline complete. Yet the evidence of history shows that today, as never before, English children have unparalleled opportunities to secure a wide and useful education.

List of dates

1698   Foundation of the Society for the Propagation of Christian Knowledge (S.P.C.K.), which began the Charity School Movement.

1762   Publication of *Émile* by Jean Jacques Rousseau.

1779   Non-conformists were allowed to teach.

1780   First Sunday School founded in Gloucester by Robert Raikes.

1803   Publication of *Improvements in Education* by Joseph Lancaster, describing the monitorial school.

1805   Pestalozzi opened his experimental school at Yverdun, Switzerland.
Eldon's judgement: grammar schools were prevented from widening their curriculum beyond the classics.

1807   Samuel Whitbread's Parochial Schools Bill proposed elementary schooling for the poor.

1810   The British and Foreign School Society was created to establish non-conformist elementary "British Schools".

1811   The National Society was founded to set up Church of England "National Schools".

1816   Robert Owen opened his infant school in New Lanark.

1819   The Charity Commission Report, presented by Henry Brougham, suggested new measures to provide education for poor children.
Hazelwood school was opened by the Hill family.

1824   The Infant School Society was founded by Robert Wilderspin.

1828   Thomas Arnold elected Headmaster of Rugby School.
Repeal of the Test Acts allowed new opportunity for non-conformists.

1832   The Reform Act enlarged middle-class franchise.

1833   The Oxford Movement began a revitalization of the English
        Church and its interest in schools.
        The first state grant of £20,000 was awarded for elementary
        school building.
1839   The Committee of Council for Education was formed, with
        James Kay-Shuttleworth as secretary.
1840   Battersea Normal School founded by Kay-Shuttleworth.
        Her Majesty's Inspectors of schools appointed.
        The Grammar Schools Act ended limitations on their
        curriculum.
1841   Cheltenham College, a model for the proprietary public
        school, was founded.
1843   A Factory Act introduced the "half-timer" system of
        schooling.
        The Governesses' Benevolent Institution opened.
1844   The Ragged School Union was founded.
1846   The pupil-teacher system was introduced.
        Lancing College, first of the Woodard Schools, was founded.
1848   Queen's College, London, opened.
1850   North London Collegiate School founded by Frances Buss.
1853   The Science and Art Department was reformed.
1854   The first English kindergarten, on the Froebel pattern, was
        opened.
1856   The Education Department was formed by the government.
        Tom Brown's Schooldays, by Thomas Hughes, was
        published.
1858   Oxford and Cambridge local examinations began.
        Dorothea Beale appointed headmistress of Cheltenham
        Ladies' College.
1861   The Newcastle Report surveyed progress in elementary
        education.
1862   The Revised Code introduced "payment by results" in
        elementary schools.
1864   The Clarendon Report on the great public schools.
1867   Cambridge local examinations opened to girls.
        The Reform Act gave franchise to artisans.
1868   The Public Schools Act introduced reforms at the "Great
        Schools".
        The Taunton Report surveyed endowed and proprietary
        schools.

1869   The Endowed Schools Act suggested reforms of grammar schools.

The Headmasters' Conference convened by Edward Thring to oppose government intervention in endowed schools.

1870   W. E. Forster's Elementary Education Act created the School Boards, providing elementary education for all.

The National Union of Teachers founded.

1876   Lord Sandon's Act ⎰ concerned with elementary school
1880   Mundella's Act.   ⎱ attendance.

The first Higher Grade School opened in Sheffield.

1888   The Local Government Act created County and Borough Councils.

The Cross Commission Report surveyed progress in elementary schooling.

1889   Cecil Reddie opened Abbotsholme School to begin a new progressive school movement.

1890   "Whiskey money" set aside by government to improve technical education.

1895   The Bryce Report discussed secondary education.

1897   "Payment by results" abolished.

1899   The Board of Education Act united competing agencies in state education.

1900   The Cockerton judgement declared the Higher Grade schools "illegal".

1901   Sidney Webb's *The Education Muddle and the Way Out* published.

1902   Education Act (Balfour and Morant): Local Education Authorities replaced School Boards.

1905   *Handbook of Suggestions for Elementary Teachers* published.

1906   The School Meals Act provided free dinners for poor children.

1907   The free place system for grammar schools was introduced.

The School Medical Service began.

1908   The Officers' Training Corps established in public schools.

1912   Maria Montessori's *The Montessori Method* published.

1917   School Certificate examinations began.

1918   H. A. L. Fisher's Education Act.

1919   The Burnham Committee was set up to consider teachers' salaries.

1922   The "Geddes Axe" cut educational expenditure.

1924 R. H. Tawney's *Secondary Education for All* published.
First schools broadcasts began.

1926 The Hadow Report considered secondary school organization and curriculum.

1930 Sawston Village College, Cambridge, opened.

1931 The Hadow Report on the primary schools published.

1938 The Spens Report discussed secondary schools.

1939 War: evacuation of schoolchildren began.

1941 The Green Book, the Board's plan for post-war education, was published.

1943 The White Paper *Educational Reconstruction* published.
The Norwood Report on secondary schools supported tripartite division of pupils.

1944 R. A. Butler's Education Act.
The Ministry of Education created.
The Fleming Report on the public schools.
The McNair Report considered teacher training.

1947 The school leaving age was raised to 15.
London's comprehensive school plan published.

1951 General Certificate of Education (G.C.E.) introduced.

1959 The Crowther Report discussed secondary pupils of average and below average ability.

1964 Certificate of Secondary Education (C.S.E.) proposed.
Department of Education and Science created.

1965 *Circular 10/65* defined the trend towards comprehensive secondary schools.

Suggested reading

* suitable for young readers

General histories of English education
J. Adamson, *English Education 1789–1902* (Cambridge, 1964).

W. Armytage, *Four Hundred Years of English Education* (Cambridge, 1964).

H. C. Barnard, *A History of English Education from 1760* (University of London Press, 1971).

S. J. Curtis and M. Boultwood, *History of English Education since 1800* (University Tutorial Press, 1960).

* K. Dawson and P. Wall, *Education* (Oxford, 1969).

A. Dures, *Schools* (Batsford, 1971).

* P. Gosden, *How they were Taught* (Blackwell, 1969).

J. Lawson and H. Silver, *A Social History of Education in England* (Methuen, 1973).

* M. Seaborne, *Education: a visual history* (Studio Vista, 1966).

M. Seaborne, *The English School; its architecture and organization 1370–1870* (Routledge and Kegan Paul, 1971).

M. Seaborne, *The English School: its architecture and organization 1870–1970* (Routledge and Kegan Paul, 1977).

Educational documents
S. Maclure, *Educational Documents 1816-present day* (Methuen, 1965).

D. Sylvester, *Educational Documents 800–1816* (Methuen, 1970).

W. Van der Eyken, *Education, the Child and Society* (Penguin, 1973).

* *The Education Act 1870* (document folder) (Department of Education and Science, 1970).

Some County archives publish collections of local documents:

Examples: * *Education in Essex 1710–1910* (Essex County Record Office, 1974).
  * *Kingston Children* (Kingston Borough Council, 1976).

State education

J. Bagley, *The State and Education in England and Wales* (Macmillan, 1969).

H. C. Dent, *1870–1970: Century of Growth in English Education* (Longman, 1970).

P. Gosden, *Education in the Second World War* (Methuen, 1976).

Elementary education

C. Birchenough, *A History of Elementary Education* (University Tutorial Press, 1920).

J. Goldstrom, *Elementary Education 1780–1900* (David and Charles, 1972).

P. Horn, *Education in Rural England 1800–1914* (Gill and Macmillan, 1978).

E. Rich, *The Education Act 1870* (Longman, 1970).

F. Smith, *A History of English Elementary Education* (University of London, 1931).

* P. Speed, *Learning and Teaching in Victorian Times* (Longman, 1964).

M. Sturt, *The Education of the People* (Routledge and Kegan Paul, 1969).

Secondary education

R. Archer, *Secondary Education in the Nineteenth Century* (Cass, 1966).

E. Eaglesham, *Foundation of Twentieth Century Education in England* (Routledge and Kegan Paul, 1967).

I. Fenwick, *The Comprehensive School 1944–1970* (Methuen, 1976).

Public schools

T. Bamford, *The Rise of the Public Schools* (Nelson, 1967).

B. Gardner, *The Public Schools* (Hamish Hamilton, 1973).

J. R. de S. Honey, *Tom Brown's Universe* (Millington, 1977).

E. Mack, *The Public Schools and British Opinion* (2 vols.) (Methuen, 1938).

V. Ogilvie, *The English Public School* (Batsford, 1957).

N. Orme, *English Schools in the Middle Ages* (Methuen, 1973).

B. Simon and I. Bradley, *The Victorian Public School* (Gill and Macmillan, 1975).

Girls' education

J. Kamm, *Hope Deferred* (Bodley Head, 1965).

J. Kamm, *How Different from Us* (Bodley Head, 1968).

B. Turner, *Equality for Some* (Ward Lock, 1974).

Educational experiment

E. Lawrence, *The Origins and Growth of Modern Education* (Pelican, 1970).

R. Skidelsky, *English Progressive Schools* (Pelican, 1969).

W. Stewart, *The Educational Innovators* (2 vols.) (Macmillan, 1967–8).

W. Stewart, *Progressives and Radicals in English Education 1750–1970* (Macmillan, 1972).

W. Van der Eyken and B. Turner, *Adventures in Education* (Pelican, 1969).

Index

116